kate moss

kate moss
model of imperfection

katherine kendall

Chamberlain Bros.
A member of Penguin Group (USA) Inc.
New York

CHAMBERLAIN BROS.
Published by the Penguin Group
Penguin Group (USA) Inc., 375 Hudson Street, New York, New York 10014, USA
Penguin Group (Canada), 10 Alcorn Avenue, Toronto, Ontario M4V 3B2, Canada
(a division of Pearson Penguin Canada Inc.)
Penguin Books Ltd, 80 Strand, London WC2R 0RL, England
Penguin Ireland, 25 St Stephen's Green, Dublin 2, Ireland (a division of Penguin
Books Ltd)
Penguin Group (Australia), 250 Camberwell Road, Camberwell, Victoria 3124, Australia
(a division of Pearson Australia Group Pty Ltd)
Penguin Books India Pvt Ltd, 11 Community Centre, Panchsheel Park, New
Delhi–110 017, India
Penguin Group (NZ), Cnr Airborne and Rosedale Roads, Albany, Auckland 1310, New
Zealand (a division of Pearson New Zealand Ltd)
Penguin Books (South Africa) (Pty) Ltd, 24 Sturdee Avenue, Rosebank, Johannesburg
2196, South Africa

Penguin Books Ltd, Registered Offices: 80 Strand, London WC2R 0RL, England

An application has been submitted to register this book with the Library of Congress.

ISBN 1-59609-033-2

While the author has made every effort to provide accurate telephone numbers and In-
ternet addresses at the time of publication, neither the publisher nor the author assumes any responsibility for errors or for changes that occur after publication.

Printed in the United States of America
10 9 8 7 6 5 4 3 2

Book design by Melissa Gerber
Photographs: Wire Image and Getty Images

contents

kate moss

introduction

"I don't like doing pictures as myself. I like to be made
into somebody different. I like to become someone
else. In a picture it's hard to be yourself. But when
you're pretending to be someone else, it's nice."
—*Kate Moss, 1999*

A model of imperfection. The subtitle sounds, as Kate
Moss might chirp in her South London accent,
"slaggy." But it is a description of the highest regard,
meant for the only supermodel who transcended the
usual celebrity trappings and "outsupered" them all. Not bad for a
too skinny girl from an unsophisticated London suburb.

Her profession is "model," yet there is nothing typically

model-like about Kate Moss. Physically, her slight body, flat chest, crooked legs, and misshapen teeth render her far from what most consider ideal. Her rebellious nature, slouchy indifference toward fame, and slapdash approach to style shatter every expectation of what a supermodel should be. Fashion editors and pop-culture pundits claim that Kate Moss opened the door for future nontraditional models—but if that is truly the case, then why are we still fascinated with the waif from Croydon, England?

To simply say that Kate Moss changed our standards of beauty is incorrect; our standards changed, and Kate personified them. She represented what had altered within us, and we related to her, accepted her. We wanted more.

In the end, it is not Kate Moss the model who resonates strongly with us, but Kate Moss the contradiction: accessible and unapproachable, vulnerable and strong, real and fantastic, delicate and fierce, sexual and androgynous. Her strangely unconventional beauty placed her alongside the most beautiful women in the world. And years later she is still there, a reminder that in the ordinary there can be something quite extraordinary.

chapter 1:
taken by storm

An airport is a sea of people, a cross section of society. Businessmen hurriedly glance at their watches, grip their briefcases, and begin sprinting. Pilots and attendants roll along with their smart carry-ons, chatting politely on their way to the lounge. A few cantankerous passengers scream at nervous airline employees. Babies wail. Children squabble. The elderly, middle-aged, teenaged, short, squat, leggy, silent, and laughing merge into an indistinguishable swarm, each person in a separate sphere of existence with one common goal: to reach a desired destination.

At a New York airport in 1988, something revolutionary was about to happen. But the moment was lost on Kate Moss, a restless fourteen-year-old enduring what would hopefully be the end

Looking casual, Kate Moss departs Los Angeles International Airport after a flight from New York in December 1994.

of a three-day layover with her younger brother, Nick, and father, Peter. As far as Kate was concerned, her revolution had already happened in the Bahamas on holiday, when she had decidedly lost her virginity to a boy there rather than waiting to give it up to some "nasty bloke" from her hometown. The brother/sister/father bonding getaway had been arranged by her father, a travel agent for Pan Am, who was at the ticket counter negotiating his way onto the next flight to London.

Sarah Doukas, owner of a fledgling fashion agency, stood at a pay phone in JFK International Airport in New York. After booking models for the IMG agency in her native London, Doukas had longed to start her own company, and her short-lived academic career had finally been put to use: she had once roomed with Lindy Branson, daughter of Sir Richard Branson, the megamillionaire behind the Virgin Group. The elder Branson had agreed to help finance Doukas's agency, and in 1987 Storm Models had been born. The only thing Doukas needed now was models. A former model herself, she knew that she couldn't wait for tomorrow's faces to show up in her office—she had to find them herself: on the street, at the grocery store, and even in the airport. Unfortunately, the scouting trip that Doukas and her brother, Simon Chambers, had taken to New York City had been fruitless, and the disheartened siblings readied themselves for an empty-handed return to London. But as Sarah Doukas's eyes scanned the thick crowd, they focused on a remarkable face that appeared momentarily, before being swallowed up again by the multitude of travelers. With high cheekbones and wide-set, mirrorlike eyes, this face wasn't merely pretty—it was *unusual*. In an instant of extreme lucidity Doukas realized that this face was *alive*; it had a personality, a tale to tell.

A year earlier, Kate's parents had divorced. The painful split had torn the family in half, leaving Nick to reside with Peter while Kate stayed with her mother, Linda. They all lived in Croydon, an industrial southern suburb of London, where Kate bided her time as an uninterested student at Riddlesdown High, a rather rough public school. Kate never did her homework and viewed school as her primary social time. Having developed a taste for mischief, she spent her school days "going to people's houses and stealing their mum's liquor. On the way to school. Anytime. Some bloke would have brought it in his bag from his dad's stash—we'd smoke and drink Super Tennants. I was smoking pot then, too." It was not juvenile delinquency so much as teenage rebellion, pushing the boundaries just to see how far they would stretch. This was due, in part, to the disintegration of her parents' relationship, which had led to a lack of family supervision.

"Literally, my parents let us do what we wanted," she said. "I was smoking when I was thirteen in front of my parents, and drinking. I'd have parties where I'd come in at three o'clock in the morning because someone chucked me out then. It's actually worked to my benefit, because you end up thinking for yourself because you know you're not rebelling against anything."

Kate's lackadaisical attitude and penchant for naughtiness were not tempered by the responsibilities of part-time work. During a brief stint working at a toy store, counting rubber spiders, Kate was lured away by a higher-paying job at a carnival. After calling in sick, she was spied by her boss at the carnival and promptly fired.

The Moss family was in luck. The flight had three remaining available seats: one in first class, one in business class, and one in economy class. Peter and Nick took the posh seats, leaving Kate in coach. Normally, Kate would have preferred riding up front, but it didn't matter—at least the trip was finally back on schedule.

Sarah Doukas was in luck as well. The face that she had noticed and lost earlier re-emerged at the boarding gate, and then was on her flight. Simon, Sarah's brother, approached Kate after takeoff, armed with a teenage fashion magazine and the question: "Have you ever thought about modeling?"

Kate had, but she had been too humble to pursue it. She had cast the thought off as unrealistic, almost boastful. "People would say, 'Oh, you should be a model,' or something like that. But I'd never really considered it," Kate later recalled. "In fact I thought it was quite vain to say, 'I want to be a model.' On a holiday I'd taken at an earlier time, I met a girl who said she wanted to be a model, and I was like, 'Oh, my God! I would never say that!' "

Back home, Peter Moss was ambivalent about the offer. "When Simon approached Kate, I was taken aback," he said. "I'd never thought of my daughter as being extraordinary, but, thinking back on that holiday, someone did comment that they thought I was a dirty old man for having such a young, pretty wife! I thought, well, if she wants to give modeling a try, why not?" Linda Moss was convinced that her daughter's encounter had been part of a hoax—the "Have you thought of modeling?" scam in which hopeful girls are fed dreams of stardom in exchange for hefty, up-front fees. Nevertheless, at Kate's insistence

Linda accompanied her daughter to the Storm office, where Doukas snapped some Polaroids and sent Kate on her first casting calls. Exhausted after a day of escorting her daughter around

Kate Moss and model Michael Bergin appear at the Calvin Klein Shop in Manhattan's Macy's store in 1994.

London, Linda advised Kate that future auditions would be on her own. Determined and showing an uncharacteristic amount of patience, Kate continued to make the rounds.

The next week, the Storm agency booked Kate's first shoot for teen magazine *Mizz*. The experience was less than spectacular. Instead of donning couture clothing, Kate covered her face in skin cleanser. "I was late and so nervous," Kate remembered. "I wasn't booked again, but not because I was late. I think it was because I wasn't pretty enough." But Doukas, convinced that she had finally found her gem, carefully watched over her protégée and continued sending her to casting calls.

As Kate dabbled in modeling, youth culture in Great Britain began to shift. The northern city of Manchester, England, had historically defined the British indie-rock scene, partly due to native son Tony Wilson, the promoter and club owner responsible for cultivating the melancholy sounds of Joy Division and New Order. Populated by starving artists and college students, Manchester was the incubator for the counterculture later christened "Madchester." The emerging designer drug Ecstasy, imported from the dance mecca on the Spanish island of Ibiza, fueled the scene with endless energy. All-night underground warehouse parties known as "raves" fed off the potent combination of drugs and the frenetic synthesizers and tribal-like rhythms of the DJs' house music. When raves were eventually outlawed and ravers were forced into a more structured club atmosphere, Tony Wilson's Hacienda club in Manchester surfaced as the "it" spot. The Stone Roses and the Happy Mondays (part of Wilson's Factory label) paved the way for Madchester's resurrection of '60s psychedelia—the Roses with their jangling guitar pop and the Mondays with dance beats, sampling, and hip-hop elements. The Mondays openly embraced drug culture and earned a notorious reputation by handing out drugs at the door to their bacchanalian shows. Day-Glo colors, worn by the dusk-till-dawn ravers, dotted Manchester's gray, muddy landscape, illuminating it with tripped-out youthful bliss.

The Madchester scene blossomed beyond northern England, propelled across the country by a new breed of periodical: the style magazine. These magazines covered all aspects of pop culture—fashion, music, sports, and celebrity—packaged with cutting-edge photography and graphic design. *The Face*, launched in 1980 by Nick Logan, excelled at identifying trends and spreading them across Great Britain. This bible of cool was a grass-roots publication, so it had no connections through which to borrow clothes, no well-known photographers, and no glossy

Kate Moss in the Calvin Klein show during Fall Fashion Week 1994 in Manhattan

pictures of highly paid models. As a result, it earned a great amount of credibility. The magazine's experimental philosophy attracted up-and-coming artists and photographers, giving them the opportunity to free their work from commercial restraint.

Corinne Day, like Sarah Doukas, was a former model who felt more comfortable behind the camera than in front of it. A self-taught photographer inspired by the neorealism of the decade, Day pioneered an organic, raw, and sometimes gritty photography style that would later be defined as "grunge." Day wanted to capture the essence of her subjects, to evoke personality rather than obscure it with makeup, lighting, and expensive clothing. Although Day's work eventually graced the pages of commercial publications, she always gravitated toward what she considered to be "real" images. At times criticized for stripping romanticism and glamour out of photography, she has also been credited with bringing a refreshing frankness to the art.

In 1990, Day sought a muse who would represent the freestyle bohemian spirit of the time—familiar yet unusual, relatable yet uncommon. She found her among the Storm portfolio pages. Instantly, Day felt a connection with Kate. "I liked her as soon as I saw her," said Day. "I think there was a bit of narcissism there because she was five foot seven inches and skinny like me. I'd been tortured at school for my shape, and had a hard time for it as a model. I thought she'd have some of the problems I've had, and wanted to help."

Kate perfectly embodied the British youth zeitgeist. Day snapped a portrait of a T-shirt-clad Kate in a drab London subway station, which was published in the March 1990 issue of *The Face*. Phil Bicker, the magazine's art director at the time, saw Day's images of Kate and knew he was looking at *The Face*'s new cover girl. "She [Kate] was completely against the whole modeling thing—very young and fresh," he recalled. "It just seemed right for the time." Two months later photographer Mark Lebon shot Kate wearing a head wrap and clutching a soccer ball for her first cover of the magazine.

That cover was a start. Kate began working primarily for *The Face*, often for little or no pay. Soon Day collaborated with her teenage ingenue on a shoot that resulted in Kate's biggest early break. Shot on a day trip to the beaches of Camber Sands, the photo landed on *The Face*'s July 1990 cover, its "Third Summer of Love" issue. Kate's crooked-tooth grin beamed from the picture, and the interior editorial pages included a shot of the rail-thin, topless model, in a feathered Indian headdress. Although the shoot appeared to be unstyled—no makeup, no primping, no designer clothing—it radiated the exuberance that had invaded British pop culture. Day cited music—particularly the Stone Roses and the Happy Mondays—as the inspiration behind the pictures.

The success of *The Face*'s "Third Summer of Love" feature led to regular collaborations between Kate and Day for future issues. According to Kate, "It was a really exciting time. I was working with Corinne. We were really close friends. I ended up living with her for a while and we'd just hang out all the time—and talk about fashion and what we were going to do and draw pictures. She had very strong opinions and very strong ideas about what she wanted to do. We did lots of the images that she wanted to do. And I think she did succeed in changing things a bit."

Day continued to photograph Kate in decidedly familiar settings: running down a freezing beach in Bournemouth, lounging about London, or relaxing in Day's apartment. "I was quite shy, believe it or not, then," explained Kate. "I was definitely more aware about my body, didn't want to take my clothes off. When I was fifteen, with Corinne, I cried. I was so self-conscious! We used to fight all the time. Those shoots would take weeks and weeks. Nobody was getting paid—it was in my school holidays."

The pictures were spontaneous and natural, images of a shy,

giggling girl blushingly holding a sun hat over her naked body or wearing a battered jacket, with her eyes closed, serene as an angel. They could easily be mistaken for an adolescent diary of the future fashion icon, but according to Kate it was all part of an act. "But I was only fifteen then. I didn't have any style," she claimed. "They styled me. It was completely contrived—you know, hunch over, whatever. I didn't want to take my top off, I didn't have tits and stuff. The pictures were about fashion, not documentary." Kate's cool slacker style was credited to Melanie Ward, who worked with Day as a fashion stylist. The two scoured flea markets and secondhand stores, partly looking for unique finds, and partly because they couldn't afford anything else.

"I still love those pictures," Kate later reminisced, "they're still some of my favorites even though I look so ugly in some of them. That topless one—I'd left school by then, but my brother really caught it. All of his mates were going, 'I've seen your sister topless!' I can appreciate it now—it was a great picture. But at the time, I was like, 'Corinne, how could you give them that picture of me looking so gross with my flat tits!'"

"I loved her attitude," Day remarked. "She was just this really cocky girl from Croydon. She wasn't like a model. She was naive in some ways, but very streetwise and quite grown-up in others."

Kate also noted, "It captured what was going on in England at the time. It wasn't eighties glamour. It was about the street. Everyone was saying, 'Let's get off our tits and have a laugh. Be more real and not have to grow up so quickly. And have fun.'"

Multiple covers and magazine editorials were not enough to convince Linda Moss of the longevity of her daughter's career. Perhaps models were high-paid jet-setters, but her daughter was neither the one nor the other. At the time, a magazine such as *The Face* was hardly considered to be professional exposure, nor was representation by a virtually unknown modeling agency.

Kate faced an uphill battle with her mother. "My mum kept asking when I was going to earn some money," she said, "and I'm trying to explain that you have to do the editorial; otherwise you'll be a catalog girl the rest of your life. She didn't understand that I had to do these pictures to earn money later."

At times, modeling did seem like a half-realized dream, but Doukas and Day supported Kate, nurtured her, and encouraged her to believe that there really was something in her modeling, difficult as it was to describe what that something was. So Kate insisted on continuing her work. But she and Doukas both realized that typical catalog work would not benefit Kate's career. Although it paid more than doing editorials for *The Face*, its primary motivation was to sell clothing, not to create an image. The goal of a catalog was to make the product look appealing enough to attract potential consumers, not to showcase the individuality and spirit of the model, or to construct an artistic statement. Kate's personality was precisely what set her apart from the standard cookie-cutter models.

However, Doukas also knew that limiting Kate to offbeat British publications would also limit her career. Bookings for major fashion shows and exclusive contracts were not generated in London, but rather in New York, Paris, or Milan. Certainly, unconventional magazines such as *The Face* could market and incorporate Kate's quirky schoolgirl looks, but the question remained as to whether the rest of the fashion world would accept her. There was no escaping the typical fashion model standards: five foot eight minimum height; a flawless, unfreckled complexion; and a rigid hourglass figure. At a shade below five foot seven, Kate hardly fit the mold with her curveless body and crooked teeth.

* * *

Around this time, the term "supermodel" was seeping into the global vocabulary. The modeling industry gravitated toward a few flagship faces—most notably Linda Evangelista, Christy Turlington, Naomi Campbell, Helena Christensen, and Tatjana Patitz. These women embodied the grand stature and breathtaking beauty that defined the traditional model. Unlike previous generations of fashion models, this new breed possessed off-runway personalities and forged its own brand of celebrity; models had stepped off catwalks and magazine pages and into music videos and television. Buxom American model Cindy Crawford was one of the first to market herself beyond the fashion magazines. Her sensual yet tasteful Herb Ritts shoot for *Playboy* and her hosting stint for the MTV fashion show *House of Style* made her a household name among men and teenagers alike, and other models soon followed her example.

Stories of supermodel life—the nonstop jetting from runway to runway, the parties, the champagne, the famous boyfriends—also infiltrated pop culture. American *Vogue* ran a now infamous story about best friends Linda Evangelista and Christy Turlington, in which Evangelista remarked, tongue-in-cheek, "We don't get out of bed for less than $10,000 a day." The quote was blown out of proportion by the media, as testimony to the supermodels' superegos. But whether interpreted as humorous or haughty, Evangelista's statement was true at least to some extent—a supermodel represented more than just a pretty face and a perfect body. She launched products and created brands, commanding compensation in the same league as actors and sports figures. The supermodel was the new celebrity for the '90s.

If supermodels were women of unattainable perfection, exactly how a tiny British girl would fit into the world of model mania would be a mystery. Doukas tried to find Kate overseas representation, to no avail. Agencies often asked to see Kate again—"when she grew into her face." However, one person was interested. Paul Rowland had recently opened his own agency, Women Management, although his office was nothing more than a desk and a phone in a New York City building. With an intimidating prizefighter build and an intense attitude to match, Rowland seemed more like a pit bull than a modeling agent. He'd spent time in the industry as a model and as a booker for a men's agency, and he wanted to start a business where the "real" money could be made—in women's modeling. But he had no models.

"The way my life works is things just come. I can never tell you what tomorrow is," he summarized his life philosophy. "I keep everything open. I keep everything moving and fluid. The thing that works for me is, I'm not afraid to attempt it. And I don't care what people have to say."

The something in Kate that Doukas saw, Rowland saw as well. The odds of Kate's achieving success seemed impossible. But the fashion pendulum—currently weighted by the usual stable of supermodels—was poised to swing in the opposite direction.

chapter 2:
slacker chic

Thousands of miles away across the Atlantic, Seattle, Washington—dreary Manchester's American counterpart—seemed dormant. But in 1991, as Kate Moss played Britain's "Summer of Love" cover girl, Seattle was primed to become the next big thing, thus setting the stage for Kate's American debut.

The 1990s marked the beginning of a dismal new era in America, where a decade-plus conservative swing in politics had spawned a generation of disenfranchised youth. Many of these children of the '80s had grown up in broken homes, victims of a skyrocketing divorce rate. Now, as adults and college graduates, they faced an increasingly tightening job market and distressing social issues that had been largely ignored in the "me" decade, such as AIDS, racism, and the renewed sexuality. Dissatisfied with the empty values of the '80s, the new "slacker" youth exemplified underachievement and sarcasm. Author Douglas Copeland called them "Generation X." Wealth was no longer a measure of success or happiness, but rather became quite the opposite—a cause of unhappiness, emptiness, and disillusionment.

Emerging cultural trends mirrored this shift in values, in music and movies and fashion. Nirvana's 1991 album, *Nevermind*, truly captured the essence of the time. The distorted, guitar-grinding single "Smells Like Teen Spirit" rebelled against blind capitalism, echoing feelings of isolation and desperation. In the following spring, the single reached the top of the charts, dethroning the resident good-time pop music that, by comparison, now sounded hopelessly passé and naive. The album's accessibility helped popularize this new sound that pop-culture mavens christened "grunge," a label later despised by the same musicians who helped define it.

The overcast Pacific Northwest region, particularly Nirvana's native Seattle, was the heart of the grunge movement. Both Manchester and Seattle had similar climates and social makeup, but while Manchester's foundation was psychedelia and Ecstasy,

Seattle's was punk-influenced guitar and heroin. Despite their differences, both countercultures influenced a new code of aesthetics based on individuality and realism—the same qualities that defined Kate Moss's modeling.

At one extreme was the supermodel celebrity, and at the other was an undercurrent of new ideals. Between the two spheres of supermodel and grunge was an increasing overlap. It was the perfect place for an unkempt, oddball beauty.

The girl who would soon define a generation lay in bed, unable to sleep. Anxiety and excited energy coursed through her, mimicking the ceaseless hum of the New York traffic outside—always moving, moving, moving, never stopping. The doctor had said nothing was wrong and scribbled out a Valium prescription. Perhaps the pills would help, but after granting Kate a mere quarter tablet, Francesca, her boyfriend's mother, had immediately repossessed them to be administered at her discretion.

A year earlier, Kate had been in London, where the drone of everyday life was punctuated by the occasional modeling job. Posing for pictures and creating fashion stories seemed more of a hobby than a real career. Yet here she was, plucked from near obscurity and dropped into New York's dizzying fashion world.

Kate Moss in the Ghost Tanya Sarne show in Manhattan's Bryant Park during 1994's Fall Fashion Week

Kate was not an amateur—her experience had given her plenty of industry knowledge—but the exponentially larger New York scene was intimidating.

Kate's life had changed. It was different, not normal. Appearing on magazine covers was not normal. Leaving high school so early was not normal. But there were a few normal things. Kate had a real boyfriend, Mario, whom she had met in England months earlier. The relationship came as a shock since she had never considered herself to be the girlfriend type. "I was quite shy at school," she confessed. "I was the girl that all the boys used to be friends with, not the girl that the boys fancied. I didn't really have a boyfriend—I was just one of the lads that hung out."

When Kate first met Mario Sorrenti, he was modeling in England and dating a mutual friend. After the friend departed for a vacation, Mario immediately pounced on Kate. "[Mario] said he wanted to take pictures of me," she laughed. "He got my phone number and rang me up to say he wanted to make me a model. That was funny."

It was a trite pickup line, but it worked.

The passion of youth and inexperience fueled their intense relationship, and the two were inseparable. Sorrenti's dark, Italian good looks had made him a model, but his real love was photography, and he channeled his infatuation through his camera lens. "It wasn't something that was conscious," he later recalled about his photographic fantasies with Kate. "I just loved taking pictures of her." The two were intertwined romantically and professionally. Their relationship would catapult them both to the top of their careers, though it was ultimately destined to become a casualty of success.

The Face served as a training ground for Sorrenti's early years as a photographer, and his influence brought Kate and her brother, Nick, together in a mutual photo shoot. Eventually, the Storm agency signed Nick on to its growing roster of male models. Like Kate's looks, Nick's features were not chiseled perfection, made apparent by his crooked nose, which had been broken in a soccer match. However, Kate and Nick were not necessarily a brother-and-sister show. The siblings' competitiveness caused a lukewarm reaction in each to the other's career, and both carried on in interviews like any typical brother and sister. "I don't know about Nick as a model," Kate later told *Vanity Fair*. "I never thought he'd be a model. But I always thought Mario would be a top photographer." Likewise, Nick quickly volunteered that Kate was not the shy, fragile doll reflected in her pictures. "When she's bitchy, she's very bitchy. That's always been in her blood," he declared.

Women Management sent Kate across the ocean to take immediate advantage of New York's opportunities, and Mario accompanied her on the trip. It made sense for the young couple to live with Mario's family, which included besides his mother, Francesca, his brother, Davide, and sister, Vandida. Francesca took on a matriarchal role for Kate, ensuring that her son's girlfriend had enough to eat and took decent care of herself.

A doting mother was not unusual. A boyfriend was not unusual. But despite this newfound stability, everything else in Kate's world was changing. The fashion industry was beginning to draw inspiration from the streets and underground culture, rather than adhering to the style edicts handed down from the designers' ivory towers. Youth counterculture movements such as rave, hip-hop, and grunge infiltrated the runways in the form of baggy pants, baseball hats, and flannel overshirts. New York was no exception, with up-and-coming designers such as Marc Jacobs and Anna Sui on the rise as America's new fashion visionaries. Sui ushered in the retrochic hippie revival, and Jacobs incorporated the deconstructionist, unglamorous style of the Seattle streets into his work. Older houses followed suit by revising their already established brands.

Calvin Klein, an American fashion powerhouse in the early '80s, was experiencing a lull in popularity, punctuated by stagnant sales. Designer jeans with emblazoned status labels seemed dated when compared with fashion's new subtlety and humility. Klein returned to his minimalist roots, which complemented the fresh, unpolished look of the early '90s. To introduce his "new" look, Klein relied on controversial advertising, as he had done with the Brooke Shields "nothing comes between me and my Calvins" nymphet campaign a decade earlier.

Fabien Baron, the mastermind image-maker and former art director of Italian *Vogue* and Andy Warhol's *Interview*, was charged with overseeing Klein's latest ad campaigns. Baron spied Kate's photo at a photography exhibition in Barcelona and cast her immediately. Klein also cast Mark Wahlberg, who was better known at the time as muscle-bound rapper Marky Mark. Wahlberg's urban street look contrasted perfectly with Kate's fragile frame. Photographer Patrick Demarchlier captured the opposing sensualities of Kate and Wahlberg, both topless in Calvin Klein men's underwear.

Kate Moss and Johnny Depp at the D.A.R.E. Benefit in Los Angeles, February 1994

Although the images evoked an erotic response, there was none of that on the set. According to Wahlberg, "Kate is a very, very nice girl. Umm, there's definitely specifics that catch my eye, but like I said, everybody is different. But . . . see, 'cause Kate is very thin . . . she's very small. I like a little bit of meat, you know what I'm saying?"

The lack of attraction was mutual. Kate recalled, "We weren't each other's types. He was this young homeboy, like really young, and he liked girls with big butts and big tits and shit and I don't really fit in that category."

"Kate and Marky both seemed to get along and like each other," remarked Neil Kraf, then senior vice president of marketing at Calvin Klein, "although I wouldn't say there was any animal magnetism there! In the TV campaign where Kate didn't have a top on, they wouldn't show the ads over here, because it was what they called 'a suggestive position.' I wasn't surprised, but those ads were aimed at MTV, and that of course was where they did get shown. I didn't see anything controversial about the two of them working together like that."

As soon as the ads began appearing, stories surfaced about Wahlberg's alleged homophobia and his involvement in racially motivated scuffles. These rumors were eventually acknowledged, but not before several New York–based antibias groups had transformed them into negative publicity for the campaign. And it was only a matter of time before Kate's flat-chested figure, which appeared prepubescent yet sexy against Wahlberg's sculpted body, caused murmurs of disapproval, echoing the response to Brooke Shields's Lolita appearance ten years earlier in Klein's jeans campaign. But the designer mapped his promotion carefully, and a brand revival was under way.

The Klein camp immediately thought of Kate as the perfect personification of the new modern look. "She has this childlike, womanlike thing that I haven't seen in a long time," Calvin Klein proclaimed of his new muse. "It's a new kind of beauty. Not the big, sporty, superwoman type, but glamour which is more sensitive, more fragile." As a result, Kate was booked for another series of Calvin Klein ads, working with Baron and Demarchlier, and she was under consideration for an exclusive contract to be the new face of Calvin Klein. The chance to represent a globally recognized fashion name with extensive media exposure was a once-in-a-lifetime opportunity.

With this high-profile contract waiting in the wings, Kate found that her next career goal was to break into the upper echelon of fashion magazines, particularly the American publishing houses of *Vogue* and *Harper's Bazaar*. Before the Calvin Klein campaign, Kate's American career had primarily existed in teen magazines such as *Seventeen*. In order to break into the elite style magazines, she would have to successfully transform herself from a teenager into a woman.

"We were very selective in our marketing of Kate," Paul Rowland, Kate's agent in America, stated emphatically. "We targeted the top magazines only." Rowland and Sarah Doukas worked hard to place Kate in fashion's top tier. But regardless of agency support, Kate found the challenge was still formidable. Generally, the industry's unwritten rule is that models who interest and inspire photographers can count on plenty of repeat work. Often, the real obstacle is finding an opportunity to work with an established photographer and, once a sitting is booked, creating an impression on said photographer. With the Calvin Klein experience under Kate's belt the timing was right, but between the sizable clique of current favorites and the intense competition from other models clamoring to get to the top, there was barely room for a newcomer.

In the fall of 1992, Hearst Publications sought to make over *Harper's Bazaar*, their flagship fashion magazine. Liz Tilberis, part of New York publishing's "British Invasion"—which included Tina Brown of *The New Yorker* and Anna Wintour of U.S. *Vogue*—was named editor in chief, and she revamped the 125-year-old magazine by combining cutting-edge fashion photography with contemporary graphic design. The magazine's new direction included the appointment of Fabien Baron, with whom Kate had previously worked, as creative director.

Tilberis brought her favorites with her from her days at the helm of British *Vogue*, including photographer Patrick Demarchlier, whose work had been published in British *Vogue* so frequently that he was known as the magazine's house photographer. Once Baron introduced his latest modeling discovery to *Harper's Bazaar*, the Baron/Demarchlier/Moss team was reunited. Tilberis was immediately taken with Kate. "The second she walked into our office," she recalled, "model editor Sara Foley and fashion director Paul Cavaco knew they were looking at a true beauty—someone whose face and attitude were the personification of the time." Tilberis agreed to use Kate in an editorial for the September relaunch issue. The resulting multi-page fashion story, "Wild: Fashion takes a walk on the wild side," featured a dramatically made-up Kate in the bohemian clothing of the season. In past pictorials, Kate had been photographed outdoors or in a common setting like an apartment, but De-marchlier placed her against stark white or gray backgrounds. Lighting added further drama, and Kate wore uncharacteristically heavy makeup that enhanced her porcelain skin, wide-set eyes, and full lips. Her attire was equally extreme; Kate's petite frame was draped in Anna Sui's retro ruffles, bound in Versace's dominatrix couture, and wrapped in leather pants. Demarchelier's breathtaking editorial photos marked the beginning of an eight-month run of Kate's appearances in the pages of *Harper's Bazaar*. The revised magazine was christened a success.

Kate worked steadily in order to gain exposure, which meant more bookings and more travel. She quickly became the model of the moment. It is not unusual for one face among a crop of new models to be dubbed "the next big thing," and Kate used her new status to garner bookings with even more fashion photography titans, such as Steven Meisel and Bruce Weber. That fall, she landed several prestigious advertising campaigns such as those of Dolce and Gabbana, Yves Saint Laurent, and Banana Republic. Kate's frequent globe-trotting conjured up glamorous images of the cosmopolitan model life, but the nonstop flurry of work had its price. The endless travel to and from locations and the increasing isolation from her friends and family took their toll on Kate, who often felt lonely and miserable. She explained her reasons for losing touch during this self-described "whirlwind phase": "[I]t felt so big—and all of a sudden to get all of this attention, and to be away from home and working all the time—was hard. I was on planes all the time. And I didn't see my friends. I cried a lot and was alone a lot. It was quite terrifying, actually."

"I started getting really nervous—panic attacks," she would also recall. "I couldn't get out of bed. It really didn't hit me at first, and then I thought I was really ill, and the doctor gave me Valium."

Although it was difficult at the time, Kate felt that the stress ultimately strengthened her ability to handle the more unappealing aspects of the industry. "It toughens you up," she insisted, reflecting on her early years. "And if you don't like it, you can always go home. You're not made to stay. I think it's really about the individual and the parents—it's more their responsibility. My parents said, 'Go for it, if you want to, but we're staying here.' I wanted to do it. I can imagine for girls who are not as street smart it could be quite tough. Girls do start quite young, and some might get led astray. It was fine with me. I wanted to go off. I don't know, it is hard for young girls in the business, but more and more today they have people from the agencies traveling with them." But at that time, Kate was alone.

Kate soon found herself representing Calvin Klein's multiple lines, including women's wear, lingerie, and jeans. The exclusive six-figure contract prevented Kate from appearing in any advertising work for other designers, but she was still free to do runway shows and editorial work for fashion magazines. It was a turning point in her career. She finally had media exposure and job security, which allowed her to be selective about what nonadvertising work she would do.

Designers began booking Kate for their runway shows. Quite different from the controlled environment of a fashion shoot, runway shows are live performances that can make or break a career. For top-tier designers, the shows serve as theatrical showcases of their collections for the upcoming season, and included on the guest list are celebrities, editors, stylists, and buyers—all in the hopes that the new clothes will appear at movie premieres, in magazine editorials, and, most important, on store racks.

Had Kate not already found success in the modeling world, her diminutive proportions would have kept her from a career on the runway, where statuesque silhouettes are typically required.

In the fashion industry, models follow stringent height and measurement standards in order to present a uniform look, and to keep garment samples at roughly the same size. However, Kate's celebrity status allowed her to break in on the runway. "In photographs, it doesn't matter, but on the runway I do think clothes look better on taller women," she said, regarding the traditional models. "It must be a bit weird for them, everyone saying this is the new look when they've got the perfect face, the perfect body, the perfect everything, and somebody who's not at all perfect comes along and starts taking all their jobs. It must be really horrible. But I don't think it will ever change that much. They won't ever be out of fashion because they're beautiful, and at the end of the day that's what people want to see—beautiful people wearing beautiful clothes."

Once again, Kate's nontraditional appearance worked for her, as did her nonchalant approach to fashion. Designers felt that Kate was more about attitude than about the tedious old standards, and that she captured the spirit of the time. "Kate's look really reflects what has gone on in the music world and that has influenced fashion," Anna Sui declared. "The spirit seems to be less 'look at me, look at me.' The same has happened with clothes, and it's now far less 'look how much I've spent.' Kate's look is very subtle—she's not like the exaggerated Amazon types that had dominated; hers is a more delicate, quiet look. For me, there's an inner beauty that has come through with the best new clothes. It is not about ostentation."

Marc Jacobs, designing for Perry Ellis at the time, echoed the thought. "I'd seen her picture in *The Face* before anyone else used her, and she looked like a little angel," he remarked. "I had the pictures on my wall, but I didn't even know her name. But then when she came in for a fitting, it was heavenly to be in the room with her, magical—she was so calm, relaxed. We didn't change anything because of her height—she walked in, wearing these Adidas trainers and a Martin Margiela skirt that was miles too long, but she'd just rolled it up to fit. That attitude toward clothes is exactly what's needed now."

The spontaneity of a live show was both exciting and terrifying, and champagne often flowed freely to ease the nerves. Kate was no stranger to this environment; years earlier, John Galliano, an upcoming British designer, had cast fifteen-year-old Kate as Lolita in one of his Paris shows. Kate had taken time off from school and stayed with one of Galliano's seamstresses. The environment had been nothing short of overwhelming. "I had to come down the catwalk by myself," she remembered. "It looked huge, like an airplane runway—I was so nervous." After the show, she had joined an impromptu gathering to watch a videotape of the show. "Someone had run off with the champagne, so me and this other person drank a bottle of scotch between us. I passed out at the table and went missing for two days. I was s'-posed to be back at school but no one knew where I was."

But now Kate had much more experience, and her low-key coolness eased her grand entrance into the world of high fashion with very little hostility from her colleagues. For the most part, the pack of already established models welcomed Kate into their nest, especially fellow catwalkers Christy Turlington and Naomi Campbell.

"When I met Naomi and Christy, they took me under their wing; we had so much fun that first season," Kate remembered. "The Galliano shows! It was amazing, like a high—the adrenaline, and 'You're on, and you're going to be this character,' and you get so into it because of the energy. It was Versace, and the parties; every night there was something you had to go to—and then you had to be up at six. I mean, it was fun!"

Campbell, a fellow Brit known for her attitude and her temper tantrums, surprisingly took to Kate. "She's very smart," Campbell said in defense of her friend. "People have this image of her as a little girl and it's completely crap. If she were, she wouldn't be where she is."

Likewise, Kate justified Campbell's difficult personality. "People have heard things about her and given her attitude, so she's given it back," she explained. "It's different for a black model in this business; she gets told, 'We're not using black models this season.'"

To her advantage, Kate had a reputation for not being an egomaniacal diva on the set, perhaps inferred from her delicate appearance. "They think of what they want you to be, and then they make you that. I'm not 'pure' or 'innocent'—it's just some of the pictures make me look that way," Kate insisted. "I'm not waiflike, fragile. I can give as good as I get. If someone's going to be a bitch to me, I can be a bitch back, but I'm not going to be horrible just for the sake of having attitude, or make other people feel small just to make me feel bigger."

Part of the refreshing attitude Kate brought to modeling was that she seemed underwhelmed by all the fuss. In an industry built on superficiality, the presence of a model who admitted to feeling ugly in the company of others was rare. "I don't feel beautiful at the moment," Kate confessed to an interviewer once. "I've got a spot on my chin. It depends. Sometimes I feel all right, and sometimes I feel, 'Oh my God.' Depends who I'm with. If I've been hanging out with Christy and Naomi for a couple of days, I feel like a piece of shit."

Although young breakthrough designers clamored to use Kate in their shows, some of the traditionalists resisted, meaning that the possibility of rejection was still very real. "When I started modeling, I didn't really care if I got rejected," she said at the time. "But now, because I'm doing so much, I kind of expect to get jobs, and get upset when I don't. Like, I went to Valentino yesterday for the runway rehearsals and I'd been confirmed for the show, but they hated me—I was just awful. They called me back and I am doing it now, but at first I thought he didn't like me at all. That was the first time I ever felt very rejected and upset. But the more success you have, the more pressure it is, because there's more pressure to stay there. Before, I was just having a laugh; now, I'm doing better jobs—I care more. You want to be good at what you do, but if you start wishing you'd got a certain job, you find yourself being jealous. As long as you're aware of it, you can stop it—you don't want to end up bitter and twisted. I mean, we are lucky."

Despite minor obstacles, Kate had secured her place within the elite inner circle of photographers, models, and stylists. How-

Kate Moss in the APLA (AIDS Project Los Angeles) Fashion Show honoring Isaac Mizrahi in May 1994

ever, she did not forget her aspiring photographer boyfriend, Mario Sorrenti, and she continued to pose for him. When Kate finally appeared on her first American magazine cover, the December 1992 issue of *Harper's Bazaar*, the magazine also contained a fashion editorial by Sorrenti, starring his girlfriend and her brother.

Calvin Klein hired Sorrenti to shoot the Obsession fragrance campaign and sent the young lovers to the isolated Caribbean island of Jost Van Dyke. The result was a sultry, sexual campaign, the most controversial yet, consisting almost entirely of nude photographs of Kate. Sorrenti insisted that Kate wear no makeup and, more important, no clothing. As Kate recalled, "Mario was like, 'You have to be naked, man—it's about purity; you have to be pure,' and I'm like, 'What's the difference if I have a pair of knickers on?' But at the end of the day, you know, he had the control."

Sorrenti also filmed Kate, material that was eventually edited into a brief commercial. The final edit featured a nubile, though clothed, Kate gazing at the camera with a whispering voice-over from Sorrenti. The commercial pushed the boundaries for Kate, who was uncomfortable broadcasting her relationship to the world. The imagery was raw and sexy, but what happened behind the scenes was anything but. "We fought the whole time," Kate recalled. " 'Obsession' is the way to describe our relationship. Calvin was very clever. He saw that. But we did the pictures and made the commercial, and that really worked. I remember hearing Mario's voice in the other room going, 'I love you, Kate. I love you, Kate.' And I was like, 'What is that?!' He was like, 'Well, it's true, man! It's true!' and I was like, 'You're mad!' "

"I think it was a bit much, actually," she would tell another interviewer. "I didn't really think about it—yeah, he's doing the pictures, great—then when it came to the commercial, and his voice-over—'I love you' and all that. . . ."

The Obsession campaign was a breakthrough for both Sorrenti and Kate. The stark, black-and-white images of Kate au naturel were mesmerizing. Rather than travel-brochure beautiful, the tropical setting was eerie and isolated—the type of place one might want to escape from, not to. A slightly disheveled Kate in such bleak surroundings created an intimate connection, as though the viewer were stranded on the island with her. Her glassy, dark eyes gazed hungrily at the camera, yet her pose seemed slightly unsure, almost docile. Her wet hair was either combed back off her forehead, or it lay in salt-water-soaked clumps around her face. In one particularly striking photo,

Kate's bare, reed-thin body sprawled across a sofa as she complacently stared up at the camera.

The campaign attracted so much attention that it was practically notorious. Kate was likened to a half-starved street urchin, a symbol of helplessness and frailty, or, simply put, a "waif."

It was a label that Kate would retain for her whole career.

chapter 3:
skin and bones

In one whirlwind year, Kate graced the pages of almost every fashion magazine in North America. Her newfound popularity in the United States even placed her on the cover of *Cosmopolitan*, a coveted spot normally reserved for her more curvaceous colleagues. Although her clothing was pinned and stuffed to create flesh that was not there, it was still symbolic of the changing times.

But one magazine cover stood out, and not because of its art direction, fashion editing, or styling. The bright red headline "Skin & Bones" was accompanied by a photo of Kate, naked, her arms crossed over her nonexistent chest. The magazine wasn't *Vogue*, *Harper's Bazaar*, or any of the regular fashion bibles. It was *People*. The feature article "How Thin Is Too

Thin?" discussed the new look that had permeated the fashion world, and questioned whether images of smaller models, particularly Kate, caused harm by promoting an anorexic look among high-school girls and impressionable youth.

"Moss and the other hot ultrathin models in the waif wave—among them Amber Valletta, Cecilia Chancellor, Emma Balfour, and Shalom Harlow—are having an effect on already weight-wary teens," the magazine observed. The tone of the article was hardly accusatory, only mentioning the latest trend and its possible impact on teenage girls. Although several other models were identified in the article, Kate's cover appearance and statements within the piece effectively labeled her as the instigator of the new craze. The story marked the entrance of the waif image into the public consciousness, and the name "Kate Moss" would continue to preface local and national news stories about the connections between fashion imagery and eating disorders for years to come.

It appeared that the media exposure that had helped Kate's career skyrocket was now turning against her. Calvin Klein, anxious to capitalize on the success of previous campaigns, saturated every magazine, billboard, television screen, and bus stop in America with Kate's image in his Obsession ads. The partially

Kate Moss takes in the Isaac Mizrahi show at Bryant Park during 1994's Fall Fashion Week.

nude images did not mix well with the emerging health debate. Women's groups decried the infantilization of women at the mercy of the fashion world; parents protested what they considered to be a sexualization of children; high-school teachers disapproved of the promotion of an unhealthy physique. A particularly contentious ad featured Kate clad in a white bikini, prominently displaying the large gap between her inner thighs. The ads were "tagged" by women's groups, who scribbled "Feed Me" and other graffiti across Kate's body.

MediaWatch, a consumer activist organization that focuses on the portrayal of women in advertising, was infuriated by the Obsession campaign. Founder Ann Simonton proposed a boycott of the promotional postcards for Klein's new fragrance. "The cards feature an image of Moss that looks like she's been busted in the lip, where she has her hand over her mouth and looks hurt," Simonton explained. "We are particularly opposed to showing images of women who are both nude and look hurt."

Shari Graydon, former president of the organization, strongly objected to the appearance of Kate looking underage and sexually vulnerable. "Although teenagers know about Kate Moss and don't read that ad as an invitation for child abuse, most adults do," Graydon stated. Her viewpoint mirrored the British reaction to Kate months earlier, when a photo shoot for British *Vogue* had touched off a media backlash. The June 1993 issue had marked Kate's first cover for the publication, with photography by Corinne Day, whose work was now in demand by glossy commercial magazines. The cover itself seemed like any other, showcasing a fresh-faced Kate in a pink and blue Chanel bustier. But the editorial inside caused a public outcry. Titled "Underexposed," it featured Kate lounging about a dirty, nondescript British flat in skimpy underwear that appeared to be off the racks of a discount store. Never before had Kate looked as thin as she did in these formfitting camisoles, slips that hugged nonexistent curves, and bras that struggled to lift barely there breasts. The magazine presented fashion's "new reality." The response was outrage.

"The pictures are hideous and tragic. If I had a daughter who looked like that, I would take her to see a doctor," declared Marcelle d'Argy Smith, editor of British *Cosmopolitan.* Smith later described the images in a 2003 newspaper article, stating, "You looked at her the way a dog lover looks at a battered, starved pup at the Battersea Dogs Home. With horror."

Other writers likened the editorial to a pedophiliac fantasy.

Women's groups, infuriated by Calvin Klein's 1994 Obsession ads depicting a disturbingly skinny and sexualized Kate Moss, retaliate by scribbling "Feed Me" across the posters.

"No pedophile would pick up that magazine," Sarah Doukas fired back, "but I'm sure they did after the press hype."

Regardless of the criticism, Kate justified her work. "The styling," she maintained, "was slaggy in a way. But I love those pictures . . . and I looked my age. Lots of women haven't got big breasts, but we still wear lingerie. . . ."

The results were damaging for Corinne Day's relationships

with both British *Vogue* and Kate, and ten years passed before she worked with either of them again. Day stated, "I thought these photographs were funny at the time—they certainly weren't the kind of photographs normally seen in *Vogue*. I had photographed Kate in her flat. I bought some underwear from Ann Summer's sex shop in Brewer Street, which is where I live. I also bought some American tan tights, I got [fashion designer] Liza Bruce to copy some T-shirts of mine so there were some designer credits in the magazine. The photographs looked cheap and tacky— everything that *Vogue* was not supposed to be. Kate had had a fight with her boyfriend that day and was crying so a few of the photographs were naturally sad. I think the press took the photographs far too seriously and read a lot more into them than what was really there."

Kate dismissed the accusations in an interview with the British style magazine *i-D*. "That felt a bit weird," she said of the situation. "I could have said something about it at the time, but that would have just been entering into their game so I didn't. I knew that the pictures weren't intended to be what they say they were, and it was really nothing—they just made a fuss about it. They're going to write things that aren't true about you all the time—it just goes over your head at the end of the day. I mean, I was like 'Oh, my God, that's really horrible, saying that.' Pedophile, uggh. But you can't let it get to you."

The association of both pedophilia and anorexia with Kate Moss marked the beginning of a rash of public criticism that haunted Kate for years to come. At some point within the media frenzy she was charged not only with causing anorexia but also with being anorexic. Making matters worse, the media now treated models like celebrities, and they expected interviews and statements. The situation made it difficult for Kate to keep silent and avoid the inevitable questions about her personal life. She had worked with photographers and stylists to articulate their vision, and now she was being punished for it.

Kate, normally quite media shy, spent the next several months fielding reporters' questions about her own eating habits, as well as about her thoughts on whether or not she inspired anorexia among young girls. Backstage at fashion shows, reporters hounded her with microphones, in search of new commentary from fashion's controversial darling.

"Women are always going to worry about what they look like," Kate explained. "When it was Cindy [Crawford] who was flavor of the month, everyone wanted to get silicone implants to get big tits. Now they say people are going to be anorexic because models have a thin body type. I don't think women are so stupid that they look at a magazine and say, 'Oh, God, I've got to be that thin to be fashionable.' As long as they feel good about themselves, they're not going to worry about what's in a fashion magazine. At least, I hope not." But Kate could only repeat herself for so long.

"At the end of the day, they're blaming me for a disease I don't have any control over. I think it's the adults putting the blame on some public figure instead of taking the blame for their child's anorexia themselves," an exasperated Kate said in a 1994 interview. "I'm sick of it. I go to restaurants and people come up and say, 'Oh, I'm disappointed you're eating.' I wasn't even the skinniest of the girls. I don't know why they picked me."

Fortunately, the fashion industry came to her defense. "Kate's just been a scapegoat of a fashion trend," Fabien Baron insisted. "It's not fair to her. She's a totally normal person, totally natural, unlike most of the models of the eighties that were into silicone, doing injections for their mouth, changing the color of the hair, and burning everything. Nobody cared about that."

Kate grew increasingly frustrated. In a later interview, she reflected on the media frenzy, and on how it felt to be a target. "At first, I got really defensive," she remembered. "I was like,

Kate Moss in the Todd Oldham show at New York City's 1994 Fall
Fashion Week

'What are they talking about?' It was upsetting, absolutely. I was a scapegoat. The media had to put responsibility on somebody, and I was chosen. They felt free to say that, because someone was thin, they were anorexic, which is ridiculous. And just because one person brought it up, then everyone was like, 'Oh, yeah! She must be anorexic.' And no matter how much I say over and over and over again that I'm not, they don't want to hear it. They want the opposite to be true. And that's even more upsetting."

Kate's public image wasn't the only victim of her popularity. In late 1993, her relationship with Sorrenti began to unravel, possibly because of both of their hectic schedules. The emotional distance between them had been growing for some time, and Kate became increasingly vague about their status. "Um . . . well, we're just sort of having a break. He lives in London, and I live in Paris," she cagily answered in an interview. "I dunno. You know how it is—relationships." After the two had officially separated, Kate offered little explanation, although she hinted that Sorrenti's desire for marriage and children was one factor.

To protect her increasing income, Kate had become a tax exile, which limited her number of trips back to Great Britain. She kept an apartment in Paris for the show season and another residence in New York, but she didn't have a permanent home base. "I'm not telling you!" she shrieked in response to an interview question regarding her living arrangements and their financial benefits. "I can't really: the tax man will be after me. I don't talk about money—it's completely insensitive. You get ridiculous amounts of money to do ridiculous things, you know, and if you talk about it to normal people, they're just, like, 'Fuck, why weren't we born beautiful?' That's what somebody said to me the other day. I mean, I do work hard, but it's a different kind of work. I don't like talking about it, though."

Kate was alone again, but not for long. In the fall of 1993, Kate attended the Council of Fashion Designers of America (CFDA) Awards, which are considered to be the Academy Awards of the industry. Calvin Klein was slated to receive the prestigious women's designer of the year award for the successful revival of his company, and Kate attended the ceremony in New York to support him. During postceremony festivities at Cafe Tabac, the trendy bistro, Kate met actor Johnny Depp. He had recently finished shooting *What's Eating Gilbert Grape*, the film that was later regarded as a breakthrough for both Depp and his young costar, then fourteen-year-old Leonardo DiCaprio.

According to Kate, she and Depp were together the instant they met. "I knew from the first moment we talked that we were going to be together," she declared shortly after their introduction. "I've never had that before. He's sweet." It marked the beginning of an intense five years for both celebrities and propelled Kate to a new level of fame.

chapter 4:
superwaif

If Kate Moss was the black sheep of the modeling world, Johnny Depp was certainly the black sheep of the film industry. A high-school dropout from Owensboro, Kentucky, Depp spent much of his youth chasing a rock star dream, and his band, the Kids, made it all the way to Los Angeles. But when the band prematurely broke up and Depp was reduced to selling pens over the phone, his friend Nicolas Cage suggested Depp try his hand at acting.

After bit roles in a few films, including *Nightmare on Elm Street*, Depp was cast as Officer Tom Hanson on the popular television drama *21 Jump Street*. His tough attitude on the show, combined with his pretty-boy good looks, earned Depp prime real estate in the school lockers and on the bedroom walls of teenage girls across America. But instead of relishing his new status as a sex symbol, Depp despised it and compared his time at *21 Jump Street* to indentured servitude, even trying to get out of his contract. "I offered to do a year of the show for free," he said. "I hate sounding like, 'Oh, I'm on television and they're paying me a load of money, poor me,' but I would have done two years for free to get out of there. They were trying to turn me into Menudo, into the New Kids on the Block. I couldn't play that game. I would rather shrink back into everyday life than get stuck being that."

Once unshackled from the show, Depp immersed himself in unusual, offbeat movie roles. *Cry-Baby*, a sharp satire of teen culture directed by cult favorite John Waters, was Depp's first starring vehicle, followed by Tim Burton's darkly comic *Edward Scissorhands*, which provided Depp with his big break as the love-starved, misunderstood title character. Depp's frequent collaborations with avant-garde directors distinguished him as an actor who preferred to challenge himself creatively rather than stick with formulaic, paycheck films.

"I'm not 'Blockbuster Boy.' I never wanted to be. I wasn't looking for that," Depp insisted. "I mean, it would be nice to get a whole shitpile of money so you can throw it at your family and

Kate Moss in a Todd Oldham show in Manhattan's Bryant Park, October 1995

friends. . . . I just don't know if movies can ever be considered art, because there's so much money involved. It's all about commerce. I don't think art can come from that place. But I aspire to be an artist someday. Maybe I'll be seventy. I don't know if it will come from being in a movie, though."

But the import and complexity of Depp's talent was often overshadowed by his brazen, rebellious, and occasionally destructive behavior. Rumors of heavy drug experimentation in his youth and tales of his turbulent love life provided endless fodder for the tabloids. Married and divorced by the age of twenty, Depp was known for his hasty engagements and abrupt breakups—to fellow actresses Jennifer (*Dirty Dancing*) Grey, Sherilyn (*Twin Peaks*) Fenn, and Winona (*Heathers*) Ryder—earning him a reputation in the media as a moody, volatile *artiste*.

Late 1993 was a particularly dark period for the actor, and he spent much of it in a self-destructive, alcoholic haze. His engagement to Winona Ryder, a relationship that Depp had famously commemorated with a "Winona Forever" tattoo on his right bicep, was agonizingly falling apart. Then, in October, actor River Phoenix died of an apparent drug overdose outside Depp's Los Angeles night club, the Viper Room. The shocking demise of the talented young actor haunted Depp, and because he co-owned the club where it had occurred, the media erroneously associated him with the suspicious circumstances of the death. "When River passed away, it happened to be at my club," Depp bitterly recounted. "Now, that's very tragic, very sad, but they made it a fiasco of lies to sell fucking magazines. They said he was doing drugs in my club, that I allow people to do drugs in my club. What a ridiculous fucking thought! Hey, I'm going to spend a lot of money on this nightclub so everyone can come here and do drugs. I think that's a good idea, don't you? We'll never get found out. It's not like this place is high profile or anything, right? That lie was ridiculous and disrespectful to River."

When critics praised Depp for his portrayal of the title character in *What's Eating Gilbert Grape*, he had to trust their assessment of his work; he never actually watched the film, because he thought it would unearth too many memories from this painful time.

Depp passed up what would become Tom Cruise's role in *Interview with the Vampire*, as well as Keanu Reeves's role in *Speed*, in order to play Ed Wood, the cross-dressing Hollywood eccentric, in a film that reunited him with director Tim Burton. As they finished filming in early 1994, Depp's relationship with Kate intensified. Gossip columns eagerly documented the physical chemistry between the two, detailing their deep kissing and passionate groping, which occurred at various New York City hot spots. The press made the romance official several weeks later, when Kate appeared with Depp in Los Angeles for the preview of his antidrug film, *Banter*.

Depp was eleven years older than Kate, but they had a lot in common. Both had grown up in broken homes, a situation that deeply affected the two of them and possibly resulted in their simultaneous fear of and desire for love. Neither played by the rules set by their respective professions, proving that models did not have to look like Barbie dolls and actors did not have to star in action flicks. Just as Depp wanted to create art through films, Kate wanted to create art through fashion photography.

"She said he's a very nice chap," Kate's father commented on his daughter's new love. "She seemed to be quite keen on him. Kate's not a silly person. She knows what she likes. And he apparently has been quite nice to her. Johnny Depp is not too dissimilar from Mario."

Depp exerted a strong influence on Kate, further cultivating her tastes in music and literature. His love for the Beat

Generation writers inspired Kate to read his favorite novel, Jack Kerouac's *On the Road*. Depp introduced her, both literally and figuratively, to Iggy Pop and Johnny Cash, and he often managed to get her away from the upscale fashion world. When Kate and Depp first met firearm-loving, drug-addled journalist Hunter S. Thompson, they were in Aspen on a skiing vacation with Kate's mother. "[Thompson] zeroes in on faults and good points immediately," Depp remembered. "I was with Kate, and I think he went straight for the romance jugular—shit like whether I beat her enough. I probably told him, 'Yeah, she gets a severe beating.'"

As an outsider to the business, Depp had plenty to learn about the fashion world.

"I said to him, 'Have you ever been to a fashion show?'" Kate recalled. "I told him about John Galliano, because he's such a good friend of mine and he's so genius. 'You should come,' I told him. I wouldn't ask him to go to any other show. The other boyfriends go. Naomi's. And Linda's. And Christy's. And Helena's . . ."

When Depp finally attended a show, Kate was both surprised and excitedly embarrassed. "When I did the Isaac Mizrahi show in L.A., Johnny was there and it was the first time he'd ever seen

Kate Moss and Calvin Klein at the Costume Institute Gala at the Metropolitan Museum of Art in Manhattan in December 1995

a show. I was like, 'Pleeease, don't come.' The show itself was the most ridiculous I've ever done because it was this fan-ta-stic, faaabulous, dadadaaaa . . . It was fun, but it was just knowing he was out there, and I cared what he thought about my job."

Up to this point, Kate's celebrity status had been limited primarily to the fashion world; despite the article in *People*, most average citizens didn't know her name and might not have recognized her on the street. Her role as Johnny Depp's girlfriend changed all that. Being photographed for a fashion magazine was one thing, but being photographed on the arm of a notorious Hollywood A-lister was another. "The first time I went to Johnny's house in L.A. is when I suddenly realized what I was getting myself into," she later recalled. "I didn't realize it when we were in New York. I knew he was famous, but I didn't really know what that entailed."

However, she eased into the celebrity lifestyle like an expert, participating in charity events, throwing parties, and attending premieres. Kate recognized the power of the paparazzi, and she quickly learned when to shine in front of the cameras and when to slip behind sunglasses for some privacy. Insiders wondered if Kate would eventually leave the catwalk and pursue an acting career, now that Depp was such an influence. Many supermodels were using their name recognition to springboard into other areas: Cindy Crawford had a starring role in a feature film, and Naomi Campbell was long-rumored to be working on a debut album. Although most of these "super side projects" ultimately flopped, people continued to speculate about Kate's potential on the silver screen.

Kate *had* thought about acting, and she had read for the part of Lucy in Francis Ford Coppola's *Dracula* before she even met Depp. In a strange coincidence, Kate's future best friend, British actress Sadie Frost, eventually played the part of Lucy, and Depp's ex, Winona Ryder, starred in the film. Because she was dating a famous actor, Kate appeared to have an easy in with Hollywood, but she seemed hesitant to commit even tentatively to a future career as an actress. Depp had seen the darker, less creative sides of the industry, and he had cautioned his girlfriend about the drawbacks. "Johnny says, 'You wouldn't want to be an actress, would you?'," she reported. "He just thinks it's going from one puppet job to another," Kate discussed her future reluctantly. "I wouldn't go up for a part, and I haven't taken any acting lessons or anything. It's something you have to really want badly and work for." Her agency remained diplomatic, neither confirming nor denying any of the rumors.

* * *

The couple worked hard to keep their romance out of the media. Depp had learned the value of privacy the hard way during his involvement with Winona Ryder; both he and Ryder had been very public from the beginning about their relationship, and neither had anticipated the level to which the media would pry. Depp felt as though his personal life had been unnecessarily invaded by strangers, and he refused to make the same mistake twice. "My relationship with my girl isn't something I'm going to discuss with anybody, especially a guy with a tape recorder," he insisted to a reporter when asked about his new love interest. "No matter how much I like them . . . Whether Kate and I are together or not is not going to save anybody's life. It's nobody's business but mine or hers. I'd rather come out in the press and say I'm [screwing] dogs, or goats, or rats than attempt [to rely on them to] write anything real about my relationship."

Only on rare occasions would Depp mention Kate, and then it was usually to dismiss the anorexia rumors. "She eats like a champ," Depp reported during the waif controversy. "She really puts it away. Why punish somebody because they have a good metabolism? Because they digest their food better? It doesn't make any sense."

Depp altered, but did not remove, his "Winona Forever" tattoo—a bold move for someone who considered his tattoos to be badges of honor. "I think of my tattoos like a journal," he once explained. "To have it ["Winona Forever"] removed, or erase it, is to try and say it never happened. If I alter it in some way, make it funny—put her next boyfriend's name on top of it, say—it would still be honest." Kate had to settle for a right bicep that read, "Wino Forever."

Recent earthquake damage in Hollywood had left Depp without a permanent home, and both he and Kate found comfort in their bohemian hotel lifestyle. In Los Angeles, the Chateau Marmont or the Hollywood Roosevelt were Depp's preferred haunts; in New York, the Mark Hotel. It was at the Mark that what would become one of the most infamous scenes in their relationship unfolded.

On September 13, 1994, after Depp and Kate had retired to Depp's suite for the evening, the hotel guard heard a commotion. Upon arriving at Depp's door and seeing a broken picture frame in the hallway, the guard threatened to call the police if Depp didn't leave the premises. "The guy was a little froggy," Depp recalled. "He decided that he was going to 'let me get in the famous guy's face.' I don't really take too well to that." Depp

Johnny Depp and Kate Moss at the premiere of *Don Juan DeMarco*, April 1995

offered to pay for damages, but he refused to leave. Then the police were called, and Depp was hauled off to jail.

The police report detailed that in the one-man brawl, Depp was responsible for, among other items, two broken seventeenth-century picture frames and prints, a china lamp stand, a Chinese pot, a shattered glass tabletop, broken coffee-table legs, broken wooden shelves, a shattered vase, and a cigarette burn on the carpet. Ironically, Roger Daltrey of the Who—a veteran hotel trasher—was trying to sleep through the ruckus in the room next door. "On a scale of one to ten," Daltrey dryly remarked, "I give him a one. It took him so bloody long. The Who could have done the job in one minute flat."

Eventually, Depp was released on the condition that he pay nearly $10,000 in damages and guest fees, and that he stay out of trouble for at least six months. But that punishment was a mere formality when compared to the media fallout. The hotel-room trashing had made headlines, further cementing Depp's reputation as an idiosyncratic rebel. And because of Kate's presence during the incident, the media speculated that an argument between the two had caused Depp's tantrum, while police suspected that Depp had been drunk or high. Kate would not comment on the situation, and Depp said as little as possible. He did, however, repeatedly insist that Kate was not involved.

"There's one thing I do want to clarify," he said firmly in a later interview. "It had nothing to do with an argument with Kate. It had to do with me."

However, he gave no other suitable explanation for his troubling behavior, even blithely remarking to an interviewer that he had been trying to smash a bug in his room. "It wasn't a great night for me," Depp said. "I'm not trying to excuse what I did or anything like that, because it's someone else's property and you gotta respect that. But you get into a head space, and you're human."

Shortly after the incident at the Mark, the couple attended a Pediatric AIDS Foundation carnival where they manned a hockey booth and assisted children with the game; a week later, they attended the premiere of *Ed Wood*, arm in arm, smiling.

By now, the tabloids had elevated Kate to fiancée status, especially after Kate had supposedly signed her name "Kate Depp" at a hotel register, which she later laughed off in an interview. Depp denied the rumors of marriage and engagement: "I can guarantee you that if I woke up one day with a wild hair up my ass to get hitched, there wouldn't be invitations. We'd run out and do it."

chapter 5:
celebrity

I n January 1995, Kate celebrated her twenty-first birthday. "Johnny said, 'We're just going to dinner,'" she recounted. "He's like, 'Put a dress on,' and I'm like, 'I haven't got a dress.' So I had on this satin dress, down to the floor, and he got the scissors and he's, like, cutting it up to the knee, literally, while we're walking out the door. I'm wearing, like, red satin up to the knee, all jagged." Kate clearly loved Depp's unassuming rebel style. And they didn't go to dinner, after all—instead Depp surprised her with a party at the Viper Room. "They opened the curtains, and there was my mum, my dad, everyone had flown in from London and New York and John [Galliano] had come from Paris—it was amazing," Kate excitedly recalled in an interview shortly thereafter. "I was, like,

Kate Moss on the runway at the Costume Institute Gala at the
Metropolitan Museum of Art in New York City, December 1995

shaking—you know, when you start to dance and your legs don't work? I had to go into the office for ten minutes till I'd calmed down."

In addition to Kate's friends and family, the special guests included '70s disco divas Thelma Houston and Gloria Gaynor, whose presence may have been a private joke between Kate and Depp. On the set of Depp's last film, Jim Jarmusch's *Dead Man*, a photo from one of Kate's fashion shoots had been taped to his dressing room mirror. It was a picture of Kate decked out in a purple satin jumpsuit and a mountain of wildly teased afro hair. The inscription read: "FROM YOUR DISCO QUEEN . . . HA, HA, HA, HA. LOVE ALWAYS, KATE."

Kate actually exerted an unlikely musical influence on Depp. "I played him Barry White and I gave him disco fever," Kate mentioned. Depp's serious music days were behind him, but he still played guitar in a side project band called "P," which featured the Butthole Surfers' lead singer, Gibby Haynes. Depp's disco fever resulted in a P cover of ABBA's "Dancing Queen."

The media still pounced on what they considered to be Kate and Depp's rock-and-roll lifestyle, resulting in rumors of decadent behavior. One story described the couple in a suite at the posh

Portobello hotel in London, supposedly ordering a tub to be filled with champagne for the ultimate bubble bath; it was reported that a hotel maid mistakenly drained the tub, thinking it was merely dirty water. Both Kate and Depp denied the story, although the suite—alongside the story—was listed on the hotel Web site as a celebrity "point of interest."

Kate was approached to write an autobiography, but she was reluctant to record her life story at the age of twenty-one, which she felt was too young for such an undertaking. She finally agreed to publish a book of photos documenting her career. "Well, when the publishers initially asked me, I didn't wanna do it. But they said you can do it any way you want," Kate later explained. "So, even though the pictures were of me, I was thinking of the book as a diary of every photographer, every stylist I worked with—a diary of the last six years of fashion and photography and styling."

In July 1995, Universe Publishing released *Kate: The Kate Moss Book*, a brief history in pictures of Kate's career. Included in the portfolio were early photos from *The Face*, the breakthrough *Harper's Bazaar* editorial, the Calvin Klein ad campaigns, and previously unpublished photographs. Even an image from the controversial British *Vogue* shoot appeared. A chapter titled "For Love, Not Money" was a montage of photographs, mostly by Mario Sorrenti. In one particularly striking photo, Kate posed behind a grimy window covered with words and shapes traced in the dirt; she was barely visible, except for her haunting eyes.

Kate modestly insisted in the foreword that the book wasn't really about her, but rather about all the people she had worked with throughout her career. "I don't know why any of this has happened," she summarized. "The chain of events that followed has led me to where I am now, and I wouldn't attempt to question any of it, or ask why. It's none of my business." In the postscript she added cheekily, "I am just on my way out to dinner, to eat a massive steak and loads of very fattening potatoes, with loads of butter."

A short publicity stint, including interviews and several book signings, followed the release of the book. It was standard promotion, but it was new territory for Kate, who was accustomed to appearing silently in photographs and not being expected to speak. Due to the combination of her inexperience, the waif controversy, and the accepted egomania of the fashion world, Kate was easy prey for the press. "I did twenty-seven interviews in a single day to publicize that book," she cynically recalled. "I was just meat ready to be slaughtered. Some people said really nasty things just to get me riled up. I was laid out for them and they went for me."

Kate's real frustration, however, stemmed from the helplessness she felt when explaining her work. After all, fashion editors and photographers controlled most of her creative output. "I'm uncomfortable with publicizing myself as a model," she sighed. "I can only say over and over again, that's what I do—I'm a model, yes—and let people make fun of me."

In another change of pace, Kate did some moonlighting as a stylist for American *Mirabella* magazine, working for photographer Glen Luchford. Setting the tone for a photo shoot was refreshing for the model, who was used to taking directions from everyone else. "I had a really good time doing it," Kate remarked. "It was nice. I said: 'I wanna see it full length, and I wanna see it like this and I wanna see it like that,' and Glen listened. As a model you don't really have a voice. Two weeks after, I did a shoot with him as a model again. At one point I said, 'Glen, can't we do it like this?' and he was, like, 'Shut up.' So it just went straight back to normal."

* * *

Kate Moss in the Calvin Klein Presents Fall 1995 Collections show at
Saks Fifth Avenue in Manhattan, September 1995.

Part of the attraction of the grunge movement was its representation of life's realities—including the mechanisms used to escape those realities. Cocaine, which had been so popular in the '80s, was deemed too "Wall Street," too "rich"; heroin, in contrast, was the ultimate artists' drug. The well-publicized addiction of Nirvana front man Kurt Cobain added an air of celebrity drama to heroin use, though in actuality Cobain privately struggled to end his drug dependence before his untimely death.

Portrayals of heroin users infiltrated movies, television, newspapers, and magazines, but these depictions—of apathetic youth with glazed eyes, smeared makeup, and willowy frames— were diluted and romanticized. Fashion magazines, for whom fantasy is sustenance, featured the new look in their pages, and "heroin chic" was born.

Kate was not a drug addict. But it didn't help that in an early interview, when asked if she smoked marijuana, she responded with, "Yeah. Who's going to say, 'No, no, I don't now'? Nobody hides it anymore. It's not like a drug—people just get it out and skin up."

Though two years had passed since the peak of the anorexia controversy and Kate's eating habits no longer made headlines, once again her thin physique was under attack, this time for looking like the body of a heroin user. *The New York Times* published a special report about the glamorization of the drug that cited Kate's work as a prime example, and resulting opinion pieces in newsmagazines echoed the thought. "Moss is a very troubling figure and a prime indicator of our degraded popular culture," columnist John Leo wrote in *U.S. News & World Report*. "She is the modern female as blank, fragile stick figure. Her pictures are full of strange allusions, many of them perverse."

Additionally, the truth about Gia Carangi, New York's supermodel of the '80s, began to surface, revealing that the exotic beauty harbored a ravenous heroin habit. In Carangi's final cover shoot for *Cosmopolitan*, she had to place her arms behind her in order to obscure the track marks. Suddenly the fashion world was to blame for heroin addiction, though no one in the press could actually produce proof for such an accusation.

"Well, after I did an interview saying I smoked pot, there was a T-shirt on Canal Street [New York] with my picture on it, and it said 'Smack Addict,'" Kate stated in a later interview. "The press has said that about me for a long time. They never ask me about it in interviews—they just insinuate it." When asked how she would respond if the press were to ask her if she were a heroin user, Kate flatly responded, "What can you say? I'm not. I never have been, I never will be."

Heroin was not a part of Kate's life, but champagne certainly was. By this time, the parties were probably the only aspect of the runway circuit that she still enjoyed. "I love a Stoli tonic," she confessed. "It's my new drink. I was drinking gin, and then someone told me about gin blossoms. My math teacher used to have them—you know, when you have a red nose. The doctor said if you're going to drink, you should drink vodka."

Off the runway, fashion editors, designers, and shoppers alike paid close attention to Kate's evolving personal style. Her laid-back attitude, humble beginnings, and Depp's anti-fashion sensibilities all influenced what she wore outside the photographer's studio. Kate avoided fussy head-to-toe designer ensembles, opting for a mix of secondhand, couture, and low-key basics. The result was a cool, relaxed look that was all her own, and her effective fashion taste further bolstered her image as a style icon.

Work kept Kate busier than ever, but the constant grind of the runway shows began to bore her. During New York's Fashion Week in 1996, she took an unexpected break from the shows and jetted off to Chicago with Depp to see the latest John Malkovich play. When asked why she continued appearing in shows, Kate responded frankly: "The money. And it is fun when you have all these models staying in the same hotel. It's just that the constant working and partying and traveling can catch up with you."

Loneliness started to catch up with Kate as well. She and Depp spent time together between projects, but when Depp was on location, the demands of filming left little room for his girlfriend. He had been in overdrive for the previous year, filming *Don Juan DeMarco* with Marlon Brando, *Dead Man*, and *Nick of Time*, and now he was preparing for *Donnie Brasco* with Al Pacino. Spending so much time alone in Los Angeles while Depp was working elsewhere proved maddening for Kate, who remarked, "[It] gets so boooring—and Johnny says, 'Well, go shopping then.'" Unfortunately shopping did little to compensate for Depp's absence.

Hectic schedules and long distances may have strained Kate and Depp's relationship, but in a particularly revealing *Playboy* interview, Depp made it clear that they were still going strong: "I love Kate more than anything. Certainly enough to marry her. But as far as putting our names on paper, making weird public vows that signify ownership—it's not in the cards." He jovially commented on the things that she does better than he (model-ing, the occasional hand of gin rummy), and on her ability to sleep very lightly. He also vehemently denied tabloid rumors that he and Kate had ever had a screaming match in a New York ho-tel lobby, maintaining that they had been in France at the time of the alleged fight.

In what was perhaps a telling moment of brutal honesty, Depp thoughtfully spoke about monogamy and his past relation-ships. "I'm very true," he maintained. "I wouldn't hurt her [Kate] and I expect she wouldn't hurt me. Fidelity is important as long as it's pure. But the moment it goes against your insides—if you want to be somewhere else; if she wants to dabble—then you need to make a change. I'm not sure any human being is made to be with one person forever and ever, amen. My own parents didn't do it; my dad left when I was fifteen. And maybe in some of my public relationships . . . maybe I was trying to right the wrongs of my parents by creating a classic fairy-tale love—trying to solve the fear of abandonment we all have. Anyway, it didn't work. That's not to say I didn't love those people. I have been with some great girls and I certainly thought I loved them, though now I have my doubts. I felt something intense, but was

Kate Moss in the Sixth on Seventh Spring Collections: Versus by Versace show in Manhattan's Bryant Park in October 1995.

it love? I don't know. So now I can't say I can love someone for-ever, or if anybody can."

In spring 1996, Depp began filming the mobster film *Donnie Brasco* in New York City. Happily, he and Kate were finally able to work from the same home base, and they rented an apartment downtown in Washington Square. Although it was only for a short three-month period, Kate enjoyed the stability and the break from their usual nomadic lifestyles.

Careerwise, the year proved to be one of her best yet. She ap-peared on more fashion magazine covers than ever before, and her contract with Calvin Klein was again renewed, as it had been each year since she had signed on to represent the label in 1993. Contract revisions allowed her to appear in other limited adver-tising, including the prestigious Versace campaign. This was shot by renowned photographer Richard Avedon, a master of portrait photography. A sitting with Avedon was considered to be a top honor for any model. The Versace campaign put Kate in very lit-tle makeup with a headful of brown frizzy curls, and rather than placing her in passive poses, Avedon snapped portraits of Kate in motion, creating a sense of movement and energy.

Once he finished filming *Donnie Brasco*, Depp was off to the Mojave Desert to direct and star in his pet project, *The Brave*. Not only was the film Depp's directorial debut, it also told a story of great personal interest to him, one that hinted at his Native American roots. Depp handled the project with kid gloves, and he persuaded his friend and mentor, Marlon Brando, to star in it.

Depp maintained that his relationship with Kate was still strong, even though she was across the world in Europe for the fall runway shows. "I am amazed," he said in a publicity interview for the film. "I am doubly amazed at how great it still is. It's still new. It's still fun. It's still very naive—even though we have all the history together now and this luggage. But it's still a good time. She makes me laugh. And, man, you can't beat that South London accent." The following spring, Kate joined Depp to support *The Brave* at the Cannes Film Festival. Unfortunately, the experience was ultimately painful for Depp.

"One of the producers premiered it at Cannes, and it was placed in the competition category," he explained. "I don't like the idea of competition, so I was frightened, because all eyes were on me and I felt like a schmuck. I was surrounded by a bunch of people in that world I didn't wanna be around. But the audience stood up for the film. The next morning, all the trades cut the movie to shreds. I was in misery. It was bizarre, because the reviews were the exact opposite of the screening."

* * *

Wounded but still unpright, Depp limped into *Fear and Loathing in Las Vegas* as Raoul Duke, alter ego of gonzo journalist Hunter S. Thompson. Based on Thompson's journal of a drug-crazed road trip, even the film would prove to be nothing short of insane, as when Depp and Kate met Thompson years earlier in Aspen. Depp bonded instantly with the author, who invited Depp and his party, including Kate's mother, back to his compound. Shooting propane tanks with guns at two in the morning proved to be more than Kate's mother could handle. "She just thought Hunter was a madman and horribly dangerous, and that we should escape as soon as possible," Depp recalled. "Hunter, being a southern gentleman, went out of his way to try to make her comfortable. By the time we left, after the explosion, and no one had been badly burned and lost any limbs, she was okay."

But by the time the film debuted, the propane tanks weren't the only things up in flames.

chapter 6:
24-hour party people

I n an early interview, Kate remarked, "Everyone has that phase in their life when they're not really sure who they are—even if it's just a short one and it comes and goes." At the time she was referring to her initial life in New York, but four years later she returned to the insecurity she had thought was behind her.

The decade of the supermodel was winding down. Actresses, promoting their latest projects, were beginning to upstage supermodels by gradually replacing them on fashion magazine covers. And the peak period of a top model's career rarely lasted longer than four years. Long-term campaigns helped secure a model's longevity, but in such a competitive and fickle industry, the chances of signing an exclusive contract were extremely slim.

Even Linda Evangelista, considered to be the most "super" of the supermodels, never became the signature face behind a major brand. When British actress Elizabeth Hurley signed on to represent cosmetics giant Estée Lauder, it was clear that fashion-related ad campaigns were no longer the exclusive domain of supermodels. Some models tried to prolong their careers by breaking into the acting world, but the cutthroat competition for parts among already established actresses left few roles for a model with little acting experience. On the rare occasions that models did win coveted roles, it was often to portray models on-screen. And a beautiful face on a magazine did not always translate into a successful actress: Cindy Crawford's performance in her debut film was almost universally panned. Other models found themselves less in demand, and designers no longer tolerated their tantrums and diva behavior. The supermodel craze had resulted in an influx of more new girls each season, and any one of them could easily replace an older model, particularly one with an attitude problem. Fortunately, Kate's close connections with major magazines still guaranteed her plenty of work.

Early in 1998, Kate traveled to Cuba with Naomi Campbell on a photo shoot for *Harper's Bazaar*, where she had the rare opportunity to meet Fidel Castro. "When we got to Cuba, we

Kate Moss appears at the Bloomingdale's store in Manhattan in February 1996 to promote her new Calvin Klein campaign.

wrote to Fidel Castro to try and meet him," Kate recounted. "We wrote that we had been with Nelson Mandela. Two days later, this guy came to meet us for lunch. He was very official looking. He had hooded eyes, sunken cheeks, he was drinking Cuban coffee and smoking cigarettes, he said, 'What kind of modeling do you do?' and things like that and eventually he said, 'Mr. Castro is a very busy man, but I will see what I can do.'" Several days later, the dictator agreed to meet the supermodels. He talked to the two women about the revolution, and he signed a book for Kate. She recalled: "He walked us to the elevator, and as the elevator doors closed—he's in his army greens—he saluted us. That and the thrill of meeting him made me feel as if I was on a roller coaster. I was screaming all the way down the elevator, all the way to the car, and all the way back to the hotel where we had to do a press conference which we were late for."

When she wasn't busy meeting foreign dignitaries, Kate made time for the Christian Dior and Cerruti campaigns and for maintaining her prestigious Calvin Klein contract. She was fortunate to work as much as she did, considering that most of her colleagues had already semiretired from the industry.

*　*　*

Over the past year, the press had become increasingly unsure about the status of Kate and Depp—often referring to the volatile relationship as "on again, off again"—and by late 1997 it certainly seemed more off than on. However, no public statements were made by either party, which left the press free to speculate. Tabloids claimed that Kate had broken it off with Depp, either because he didn't spend enough time with her or because she wanted to have a baby. But none of the tales could be substantiated.

Kate did appear with Depp at the Cannes Film Festival in May 1998, where he was supporting *Fear and Loathing in Las Vegas*. The media-shy actor avoided all questions about his personal life. "We should stick to stuff that's film based," Depp informed a reporter, "until we make *Kate & Johnny: The Movie*. I'll tell you, she's a great girl and I care for her deeply. That's what I'll say about that." He later stressed that he and Kate had met at the premiere only as old friends.

Overshadowing the status of her relationship with Depp were rumors of Kate's wild partying. Stories circulated that when she was staying at the Hôtel du Cap, other guests had complained of loud music coming from her room, and that the hotel did not approve of her toting a bottle of champagne around the lobby in the wee hours of the morning. It was reported that the hotel banned her for life, though Kate's management insisted that she left the hotel of her own accord. "My room was next to the bar and their music was blaring," Kate explained. "So I thought they wouldn't notice mine, but they just got cross, and then they asked me not to wear a bikini around the hotel and it was like, *excusez-moi*!"

Kate's story may have conflicted with the hotel's, but one thing *was* certain—Kate and Depp had broken up. Now that the stability she had derived from her relationship had disappeared, she returned home to London in an attempt to fill the newfound emptiness in her life. But the whirl of parties continued. Kate socialized with the most notorious of Britain's new partyers: Oasis front man Noel Gallagher and his wife, Meg Matthews; Jade Jagger, Mick and Bianca's daughter; up-and-coming actress Anna Friel; and film supercouple Sadie Frost and Jude Law.

Kate drastically reduced her runway appearances because the frenetic pace of back-to-back shows interfered with her new social circle. Money was no longer an issue; she was established enough to rely on her contracts and fashion editorials. "That's the sick thing," she exclaimed. "You get so flippant about the

Model Claudia Schiffer, left, and Kate Moss strike a red-carpet pose at the 51st Cannes Film Festival in 1998.

money. But it was also a question of having to save myself. I got tired of feeling like Dracula. I wanted to see some daylight, and not just at six o'clock in the morning."

Now that Depp was out of the picture, the British press had a field day with Kate's string of supposed beaux. She was spied hand in hand with Evan Dando, scruffy lead singer of the Lemonheads (ironically, in 1991 Depp had appeared in the video for their crossover hit "It's a Shame About Ray"), and Kate eventually acknowledged that they *were* linked—but only as godparents to the daughter of mutual friend Lucie de la Falaise. After rumors of a dalliance with trip-hop artist Goldie, paparazzi cameras caught her sunbathing on vacation with music producer Nellee Hooper. Then society man Dan MacMillan, heir to a publishing empire, joined the list of possible lovers, and she supposedly went on a Moroccan vacation with musician Tarka Cordell. Kate wearily denied the stories.

"No, I'm not seeing Dan MacMillan," she insisted. "No, I'm not seeing Evan Dando. When you're single, everyone assumes you're dating any guy you're seen out with. It's really annoying. 'Who's she gonna be with next?' You can't be seen out with anybody! You don't want to be seen out with anybody!"

Kate enjoyed keeping the media guessing. "I actually had decoys," she later admitted. "And we'd go out and get photographed and think, 'Fuck 'em all,' but that's just mates having a laugh. They would say I was going out with one person and I would be seen out with another person just to throw them off. I've only done that once actually, because it's not good to play games."

In the meantime, tabloid chatter still claimed Johnny Depp was in Kate's life. While he was in London filming Tim Burton's *Sleepy Hollow*, the press relentlessly tracked them down, filling gossip columns with reports of the two sharing secret dinners in trendy Notting Hill and rumors of Depp's chauffeured car seen outside Kate's house in the morning. People wondered if perhaps Depp wanted to rekindle the romance. But any hopes that the two would reunite were abruptly dashed when it was confirmed that Vanessa Paradis was pregnant with Johnny Depp's child. The two had met in June 1998 after an audition for Depp's latest project, Roman Polanski's *The Ninth Gate*. The delicately beautiful Paradis had attained pop star status as an actress in France by the time she was fourteen; outside France, she was best known for her portrayal of Chanel's bird in a gilded cage, the company's successful advertising campaign. Strangely, Paradis bore a striking resemblance to Kate, with her wide-set eyes, childlike pout,

Kate Moss gets cozy with actor Rupert Everett at a 1998 awards dinner honoring Elizabeth Taylor.

and wisp of a figure. Depp made the relationship no secret. "What struck me first of all was her beauty," Depp said. "And what touched me afterward was her tenderness. I can tell you that in these days of serial marriages, Vanessa and I are a solid couple."

Depp's impending fatherhood appeared to be an unplanned event, but he quickly dispelled rumors that the child had spoiled his intentions to return to Kate. "That couldn't be more untrue," he said. "I was not put in a situation where I was obligated to do something. Obligation is no way to begin your career as a father. I would never do that to the girl that I'm involved with, to my kid. I wouldn't live that lie."

The news stung Kate like a slap in the face. Her true love had started a new life and a new family with another woman, and any chance of reconciliation was impossible. She felt erased from Depp's memory.

For the next few months, Kate plunged into the celebrity party circuit. The paparazzi played the game of "Kate spotting," snapping her picture at every premiere, fashion show, charity event, and record release party. But the nonstop social whirl took its toll on her physically, and in one of her last photo shoots of the year, with photographer Mario Testino, Kate was visibly tired. Testino set her against a plain background, and Kate was dressed in the brightly colored clothing of the season, with pink hair left over from a recent Versace show. But the clothing and the colors could not compensate for Kate's lack of vibrancy; her skin was gray and her eyes were lifeless.

By early November she had had enough.

chapter 7:
lost plot

One night, Kate quietly checked into rehab.

She was quick to deny that any drugs were involved, claiming that she had made the decision because she was exhausted from the constant partying, and because she needed a break to relax and regroup. "It was just a buildup, really. I was definitely living fast," she later explained. "It was, 'Sleep? Why? Why not go on? There's too much to do. There're too many places to go.' I was working, I was traveling a lot. I was playing and I didn't stop. It got to the point where it wasn't so much fun anymore. It all became unbalanced, so one day I just said, 'I can't do this anymore. I've had enough.' It was getting ridiculous. I was not very happy. I was

Kate Moss and Antony Langdon at the *Talk* magazine launch gala in New York, August 1999

doing things that weren't good for me. So I checked into the Churchill Priory clinic."

Her press agent issued a similar statement: "Kate's burned out. She wanted to reevaluate her life, and so she put herself in the situation where she'd be able to do that."

Kate stayed at the Priory, a $500-a-day private psychiatric hospital in southwest London, for five weeks, until right before the holidays in December. She checked in under a fake name, but the news did not stay secret for long. Soon enough, the tabloids and even the newswires picked up the story, and word traveled fast that Kate was furious with her pal Meg Matthews for breaking the story to the media.

Despite the widespread publicity, Kate was confident that she had made the right decision. "It was the best thing I've done for ages," she emphasized. "I needed to check in and ask, 'What's going on?' I had tried to stop certain things before; I had tried to get focused on other things. But I always ended up back in the same place, and it wasn't making me happy. I needed to get the focus back, and ask, 'What do I want?' Going on holiday wasn't doing it. That's not real life. I needed to do it in London."

Of course, any celebrity stint in rehab would not be complete without rumors leaking out from behind the clinic walls. It was reported that Kate had set fire to her room, and that Depp had delivered a brand-new BMW to the clinic as a gift: the former was true; the latter was not. Kate *had* accidentally started a fire on her last day at the Priory when a candle ignited a scarf she had hanging in her room. The flames were extinguished before they caused any damage, but the fire department still arrived on the scene.

And it was the manufacturers of the Mini Cooper that sent her a car, not Depp. "Suddenly, it turned into a BMW that Johnny gave me. How did a Mini Cooper suddenly transform into a BMW from Johnny Depp? Where did that come from?" she wondered aloud in a post-Priory interview. "Nope! It's not his style, a BMW." Kate did, however, note that Depp was aware of her stay, and that he fully supported her efforts to refocus.

"It's kind of like being at boarding school," she said of the experience. "I really liked it. I go back and visit people. In the Priory they believe that either you're an addict or you're not an addict, or you have an addictive personality, and there's patterns, and all addicts have the same patterns. So being in there with other alcoholics and drug addicts and people, then you realize—you see your patterns." Kate chose her words carefully, but it was obvious that she had emerged from the Priory with a better understanding of what had led her up to that point, and of how to avoid reaching it again. In order to help maintain a more serene lifestyle, she bought a quiet country home in St. John's Wood.

Her brief stay at the Priory may have revived Kate's sense of serenity, but other tumultuous aspects of her life continued. Within months, Calvin Klein decided not to renew her contract. Kate had represented the brand—which encompassed women's wear, eyeglasses, lingerie, jeans, and fragrance lines—since 1993, and her face had become synonymous with the designer's name. Though some suspected otherwise, the company maintained that its decision had nothing to do with Kate's stay in rehab, and that the two were parting ways amicably. At the March 1999 unveiling of his latest collection, Klein announced that an up-and-coming eighteen-year-old Russian model would be the new face of Calvin Klein.

Reaction was mixed. Some felt that Klein was attempting to clean up his image. Since the controversial Kate Moss campaigns, Klein had been under fire again in 1997 for running ads that were accused of simulating child pornography, even though the models used were all of legal age. But as a result of the media outcry, Klein had pulled the entire campaign and issued a public apology.

"I think he let Kate go because she went public about her drinking and drug use," an anonymous insider told the *New York Daily News*. "He should have supported her." Others acknowledged that it was bad timing, but insisted that it did not have anything to do with the Priory stay. Kate had represented Klein for nearly six years—an eternity in the fashion industry—and perhaps Klein merely wanted a change. Neither Klein nor Kate offered an official comment.

Though she initially viewed it as a disappointment, the contract's end came to symbolize a new beginning for Kate. She graced the catwalk for Donatella Versace's spring show, sober on the runway for the first time in years. The fashion community warmly welcomed her back, showering her with spontaneous outbursts of applause. "It was just amazing," Kate gushed. "I was amazed at the support that I got when I was in there. And when I came out, people knew that I was back on track. For a while I really had lost interest. Suddenly, I was interested in working again. And people could feel it. I've found out so much about myself recently. It's all been a learning experience."

"I was quite nervous for the first show," Kate told another interviewer. "It was like a whole new experience—seeing things in a different way. You can get jaded doing it so long. You can

Actresses Gwyneth Paltrow, left, and Liv Tyler, right, flank Kate Moss for a photo op.

think, 'I'm bored of this.' But going back to it after time off is almost like starting over."

In January, Kate celebrated her twenty-fifth birthday at Les Bains Douches nightclub in Paris, at a party thrown by Donatella

Versace. The model spent the night dancing and mingling at the celebrity-studded gala, which included guests such as Catherine Zeta-Jones, Christina Ricci, and Liv Tyler. Actor Billy Zane, enjoying the success of the previous year's *Titanic* as well as Kate's company, lifted her up to blow out the candles on her massive birthday cake. Her mother was by Kate's side as she rang in her twenty-fifth year, sober. And happy.

Kate was eager to return to work, and fashion houses like Burberry quickly signed her up for their campaigns. Magazines clamored to publish features on the new-and-improved Kate Moss, which wasn't easy, but Kate realized that it was better to control the story than to let the tabloids run with it. She agreed to several interviews for magazines including British *Vogue*, *Interview*, and *The Face*. The stories were intensely personal—not the type of press that Kate was comfortable with—and some aspects of her life were off-limits; she never revealed the specific trigger that had caused her to check into rehab. But in general, Kate was uncharacteristically candid about her recovery, as well as about the modeling industry. "I always said I was never going to go for it in a major way because I never wanted to go into rehab," she told *The Face*. "I never, ever wanted to end up in the position when I couldn't have a drink. Which is probably the first sign of it: 'No, I never want to not be able to have a drink.' You moderate things so you don't have to get to that point. But I couldn't keep myself in check anymore. Couldn't do it. I kind of lost the plot really there a little bit."

She admitted that during the past year she had been slacking at her job and that she hadn't been sober on the catwalk for an entire decade. However, Kate refused to play the victim, and she was quick to defend the fashion industry. "It's like when you do the shows, the first thing they give you before you go out on the runway is champagne," she stated. "I'm not saying that it makes a difference. I was drinking when I was fourteen or fifteen, when I was still living in Croydon I was down at the pub getting drunk. I don't think it's anything to do with my work. There's as much pressure in this industry as any other high-pressure industry."

The interviews also allowed her to reflect on her relationship with Depp. "He was away a lot of the time, and I'd go shopping, do that ladies-who-lunch crap, faff around. It was so boring—the most lonely, shallow place," Kate acknowledged. "I was going insane. I'm not normally a depressed person, but I brooded, got really sad—and we grew apart. And now he's got his life and I've got mine."

Depp was her one true love, Kate admitted, and to some extent she still mourned the demise of the relationship. But she was comfortable being on her own for the moment—solitude gave her the ability to focus on her emotional health. When asked about the idea of falling in love again, Kate hesitantly responded, "I don't think I've completely got over my relationship with Johnny so it's hard for me to think about being in love with anyone else. It was so intense for four years and it's still quite strange."

Once the interviews went to press, Kate spoke less about her therapy and the Priory, perhaps feeling that she had already revealed too much about herself to the public. And some of her statements were taken out of context. In her interview with *The Face*, she had bluntly described the casual use of marijuana on most modeling shoots. "In France and London," she declared, "we're allowed to smoke pot all day. After the first picture, skin up!" This statement, combined with her insistence in an earlier documentary interview that she didn't do drugs more than anyone else, created false impressions, and the press began to paint an unflattering portrait of the model: Kate really did do drugs, she was a drunk, she had been a drunk since a very young age. . . . Kate felt vulnerable and exposed.

She gingerly reintroduced herself into the social scene,

Kate Moss poses at a portrait shoot in Cannes in 2001.

though with far less fervor than before, and it didn't take long for the press to return to speculating about her love life. In June 2000, Kate's new mystery man was identified as Antony Langdon, guitarist for the band Spacehog, whom she had met through her friend Liv Tyler, who was dating (and would later marry) Antony's brother, Royston. Rumors intensified and at their peak claimed that Kate was sporting a $15,000 engagement ring from Langdon. But soon after the story ran, the romance fizzled. The ring disappeared, reported as having been merely a decorative piece from Kate's friend, jewelry designer Jade Jagger. After rumors of a brief dalliance with musician Lenny Kravitz, Kate reputedly spent Christmas and New Year's Eve with Jesse Wood, the son of Rolling Stone bassist Ron Wood, and the two were later photographed enjoying themselves on a Thai vacation in Phuket.

In March, Kate suddenly collapsed and was rushed to the hospital. Much to the tabloids' disappointment, a kidney infection was to blame, not a relapse. "Kate is living a very quiet life," read Sarah Doukas's statement. "Her hospital treatment has nothing to do with drink and drugs. Kate was in a lot of pain and had a high fever. She was in abject misery." Wood remained at her bedside during her recovery. But that relationship was also short-lived, deemed over by the summer.

In the meantime, Kate cultivated friendships with Marianne Faithfull and Anita Pallenberg, former Rolling Stones girlfriends who had battled drug addictions in the past. Both women were substantially older than Kate, and a world apart from Kate's usual crowd, but Kate viewed them both as mentors; they had lived full, turbulent lives, and they had survived.

By the end of 2000, Kate was back at the top of her game, refreshed and revived. And wanting a baby. It had never been a secret that Kate longed to have children, and now she seemed to want motherhood more than ever. "Before, I was never really around babies and stuff, but now everyone seems to be having a baby, loads of my friends," she said. "I'm broody, anyway. I love kids, but it kind of makes me think about it a lot more. If I haven't met Mr. Right in a few years, I'm going to do it, anyway. Definitely." It was anyone's guess as to who Mr. Right would be.

chapter 8:
triumphant

You smell of pee."

It was not what one would expect to hear from a suitor, but the reported pickup line Jefferson Hack used on Kate seemed to have worked. Kate began 2001 with a new beau, a more permanent fixture than the flirtations of her recent past. Hack, the editor of the new style magazine *Dazed and Confused*, was tall and slender, with mousy short hair and the classic look of a British gentleman—a sweet, geeky contrast to Johnny Depp's high cheekbones and rough-and-tumble appearance. Hack had first met Kate while conducting a post-Priory interview for his magazine, and they had kept in touch.

Mario's number one: Kate Moss at the Mario Testino Exhibition at the National Portrait Gallery in London, January 2002

Two years later, he whisked her off to the Carribbean to celebrate her twenty-seventh birthday.

Kate had other reasons to celebrate. She had signed a long-term contract with Rimmel, a London-based cosmetics company. She had also offered herself to the art world; in May, British *Vogue* invited London's rising stars in the world of fine arts to use Kate as their muse. Artist siblings Jake and Dinos Chapman, whom Kate knew already, had her sketch her own portrait, which they embellished with drawings of cartoonish severed heads. Marc Quinn cast her body into an ice sculpture that was clothed in Alexander McQueen—it was not permanent and would slowly melt and evaporate over a four-month period. "When people come to see the sculpture, its molecules will be transferred from the sculpture to the lungs of the onlookers by the process of evaporation. The viewers will literally breathe in the image of Kate Moss, consume her," stated the artist.

The resurgence in Kate's career could also be attributed to her close relationship with photographer Mario Testino. Famous for having taken Princess Diana's last portrait before her death,

In London in June 2003, Kate Moss launches a new cosmetics line as "the face" of Rimmel U.K.

Testino was considered to be one of the world's most sought-after fashion photographers, and it was no surprise that his frequent collaborations with Kate were in high demand. Although the two had worked together for years, Kate's restored focus and energy reinvigorated their creative relationship. He affectionately referred to her as his all-time favorite girl to photograph, saying, "Kate always works so hard to give you what you want in an image—and there's always this incredible naturalness." In a joint interview he turned to Kate and stated, "You work and you want it to work. Because it is work—it's not just standing there in front of the camera. For us, every shot is a problem that we have to solve. And whoever helps us solve that problem we like to work with."

In March 2002, Kate and Hack joyfully confirmed that Kate was indeed pregnant and expecting a baby in the fall. The press hounded Kate in search of a story, while Kate relaxed her schedule and bided her time with her good friend Sadie Frost, who was also expecting.

Kate's daughter, Lila Grace, was born on a Sunday morning in September. The announcement of a wedding date was expected from Kate and Hack, and columnists spied him shopping for an engagement ring. But the couple were evasive about their future plans, saying only that they intended to enjoy this time with their new baby. They eventually split, in March 2004, though the British tabloids occasionally still report seeing them together. Most recently, Kate has been spotted with actors Johnny Knoxville and Jack Nicholson.

Shortly after the birth of Lila Grace, Kate amicably parted ways with Paul Rowland and Women Management and signed on with the IMG agency, which represented modeling superstars such as Brazil's Gisele Bündchen. However, Kate still remained loyal to Sarah Doukas and stayed on the roster at the Storm agency, which had always represented her in Great Britain.

Sales of Burberry increased exponentially, and the company attributed to Kate its resurgent popularity. She also signed on to star in the fall campaign for luxury label Fendi, and she continued her contract with Rimmel cosmetics.

Then things got even better.

W magazine, which had featured Kate in photo shoots and on covers since she first moved to New York as a teenager, dedicated their September 2003 issue to her. Kate was on not one cover, but nine, photographed by nine different photographers. The title splashed across all nine versions of the magazine was the same: "The Triumphant Return of a Superstar." The cover images—from a glammed-out Venus-in-furs photographed by Juergen Teller, to a rough-and-tough homegirl photographed by Bruce Weber, to a sweet-faced cherub photographed by former flame Mario Sorrenti—keenly exemplified the many facets of Kate, emphasizing how easily she slipped into character for her work. The forty-page portfolio inside the magazine was further testament to Kate's transformation from fashion model to artistic muse. Japanese artist Takashi Murakami, known for his multicolor Louis Vuitton creations, illustrated a pregnant Kate in bright Day-Glo colors, surrounded by his trademark cartoon eyeballs. Craig McDean snapped shots of Kate as a sexy siren in fishnets and panties. A nude painting of Kate by octogenarian British artist Lucian Freud rounded out the diverse collection.

The issue summarized Kate perfectly as an artist's ultimate medium, who allowed herself to be molded, shaped, pushed, pulled, and otherwise manipulated in order to create a visual statement. The Kate Moss in each spread is at once everything and nothing. She is a celebrity, a fashion icon, a muse, a princess

Naomi Campbell, left, designer Alexander McQueen, Kate Moss, and model Annabelle Nielsen, right, attend the after party of the American Express Black Fashion Show in June 2004.

in a shredded satin dress waiting to be whisked away. Yet she is also still an awkward girl running down the cold beaches of Camber Sands, as fast as her crooked legs will take her. But perhaps most of all, she is still a gangly teen sitting restlessly in a crowded airport, basking in the glow of youth and awaiting the next flight home.

acknowledgments

Thank you to Kate

Also to:

My family for much encouragement and nurturing my eccentricities

Eric, my friend, cheerleader, consultant, and love

David and Gina, Peter and Kim, GR, Paula, Wendi, Sarah, and Brian for conversation and caffeine

Anyone who looked at me strangely and asked, "You're writing a book on *who*?"

Supporters of kate*site

notes

Introduction

"I don't like": "The Kate Moss Story," Ingrid Sischy, *Interview*, March 1999.

Chapter 1

"Going to people's houses": "Kate Unmasked," Lisa Armstrong, British *Vogue*, April 1999.

"Literally, my parents": "America's Obsession," Elizabeth Mitchell, *Spin*, January 1994.

"People would say": "The Kate Moss Story," Ingrid Sischy, *Interview*, March 1999.

"I'd never thought": "Small Wonder," Lesley White, British *Vogue*, August 1994.

"I was late": "Kate Looks 30 in the Face," Jill Foster, *The Mirror*, January 13, 2004.

"I liked her": "Fast Times—The Photography of Corinne Day," Adrian Gargett, getunderground.com, May 2003.

"She was completely": "The Making of Kate," Sheryl Garratt, *The Face*, March 1993.

"It was a really exciting time": "The Kate Moss Story," Ingrid Sischy, *Interview*, March 1999.

"I was quite shy": "Staying Alive," Sarah Mower, *Vogue*, September 2004.

"But I was only": "Staying Alive," Sarah Mower, *Vogue*, September 2004.

"I still love those pictures": "The Making of Kate," Sheryl Garratt, *The Face*, March 1993.

"I loved her attitude": "Small Wonder," Lesley White, British *Vogue*, August 1994.

"It captured what was going on": "The Kate Moss Story," Ingrid Sischy, *Interview*, March 1999.

"My mum kept asking": "The Making of Kate," Sheryl Garratt, *The Face*, March 1993.

"The way my life works": models.com/model_culture/agency_spotlight/women

Chapter 2

"I was quite shy": "Kate Moss," Avril Mair, *i-D*, December 1993.

"[Mario] said he wanted": "Kate Moss," Avril Mair, *i-D*, December 1993.

"It wasn't something": "All About Kate," Julie L. Belcove, *W*, September 2003.

"I don't know": "Kiss Me, Kate," George Wayne, *Vanity Fair*, January 1994.

"When she's bitchy": "America's Obsession," Elizabeth Mitchell, *Spin*, January 1994.

"Kate is a very, very nice girl": "Marky's Bad Rap?" Robinne Lee, *Tell* magazine, Summer 1994.

"We weren't each": "Kate Moss," Avril Mair, *i-D*, December 1993.

"Kate and Marky both": "The Making of Kate," Sheryl Garratt, *The Face*, March 1993.

"She has this childlike": "[Kate Moss] 50 Most Beautiful People," Lesley Alderman, *People*, May 3, 1993.

"We were very selective": "Little Miss Moss," Tina Gaudoin, *Harper's Bazaar*, December 1992.

"The second she walked": "A Girl Called Kate," Shane Watson, British *Elle*, July 1995.

"Because it felt": "The Kate Moss Story," Ingrid Sischy, *Interview*, March 1999.

"I started getting": "Staying Alive," Sarah Mower, *Vogue*, September 2004.

"It toughens you up": "Miss Moss," Bridget Foley, *W*, March 1999.

"In photographs": "The Making of Kate," Sheryl Garratt, *The Face*, March 1993.

"Kate's look really": "The Making of Kate," Sheryl Garratt, *The Face*, March 1993.

"I'd seen her picture": "The Making of Kate," Sheryl Garratt, *The Face*, March 1993.

"I had to come down": "Kate Unmasked," Lisa Armstrong, British *Vogue*, April 1999.

"When I met": "Staying Alive," Sarah Mower, *Vogue*, September 2004.

"She's very smart": "America's Obsession," Elizabeth Mitchell, *Spin*, January 1994.

"People have heard": "Small Wonder," Lesley White, British *Vogue*, August 1994.

"They think of what": "The Making of Kate," Sheryl Garratt, *The Face*, March 1993.

"I don't feel beautiful": "Golden Girl," Ian Parker, British *Esquire*, December 1993.

"When I started modeling": "The Making of Kate," Sheryl Garratt, *The Face*, March 1993.

"Mario was like": "A Girl Called Kate," Shane Watson, British *Elle*, July 1995.

"We fought": "The Kate Moss Story," Ingrid Sischy, *Interview*, March 1999.

"I think it was": "A Girl Called Kate," Shane Watson, British *Elle*, July 1995.

Chapter 3

"Moss and the other": "How Thin Is Too Thin?" Louise Lague, Allison Lynn, Lois Armstrong, Vicki Sheff-Cahan, Gabrielle Saveri, *People Weekly*, September 20, 1993.

"The cards feature": "America's Obsession," Elizabeth Mitchell, *Spin*, January 1994.

"Although teenagers know": "Breaking the Mold," Idella Sturino, *The Peak*, March 18, 1996.

"The pictures are hideous": "How Thin Is Too Thin?" Louise Lague, Allison Lynn, Lois Armstrong, Vicki Sheff-Cahan, Gabrielle Saveri, *People Weekly*, September 20, 1993.

"You looked at her": "Celebs to Blame for Anorexia," Marcelle d'Argy Smith, *Daily Mail*, October 2, 2003.

"No pedophile": "America's Obsession," Elizabeth Mitchell, *Spin*, January 1994.

"The styling was slaggy": "Golden Girl," Ian Parker, British *Esquire*, December 1993.

"I thought these photographs": www.corinneday.co.uk/bio.html.

"That felt a bit": "Kate Moss," Avril Mair, *i-D*, December 1993.

"Women are always": "Kate Moss," Avril Mair, *i-D*, December 1993.

"At the end": "Small Wonder," Lesley White, British *Vogue*, August 1994.

"Kate's just been": "America's Obsession," Elizabeth Mitchell, *Spin*, January 1994.

"At first, I got": "The Kate Moss Story," Ingrid Sischy, *Interview*, March 1999.

"Um . . . well": "Kiss Me, Kate," George Wayne, *Vanity Fair*, January 1994.

To protect her: "The Thin Girl," Cathy Horyn, *Allure*, May 1994.

"I'm not telling": "Kate Moss," Avril Mair, *i-D*, December 1993.

"I knew from": "America's Obsession," Elizabeth Mitchell, *Spin*, January 1994.

Chapter 4

"I offered": "Playboy Interview: Johnny Depp," Kevin Cook, *Playboy*, January 1996.

"I'm not 'Blockbuster Boy' ": "Johnny Be Good," Kevin Sessums, *Vanity Fair*, February 1997.

"When River passed away": "Playboy Interview: Johnny Depp," Kevin Cook, *Playboy*, January 1996.

"She said he's": "The Thin Girl," Cathy Horyn, *Allure*, May 1994.

"[Thompson] zeroes in": "Johnny Depp's Savage Journey," Chris Heath, *Rolling Stone*, June 11, 1998.

"I said to him": "The Thin Girl," Cathy Horyn, *Allure*, May 1994.

"When I did": "America's Obsession," Elizabeth Mitchell, *Spin*, January 1994.

"The first time": "The Kate Moss Story," Ingrid Sischy, *Interview*, March 1999.

"Johnny says": "America's Obsession," Elizabeth Mitchell, *Spin*, January 1994.

"I wouldn't go": "The Making of Kate," Sheryl Garratt, *The Face*, March 1993.

"My relationship with my girl": "Depp Gets Deeper," James Ryan, *Vogue*, September 1994.

"She eats like": "The Buzz on Johnny Depp," David Blum, *Esquire*, April 1995.

"I think of my tattoos": "Johnny Angel," Johanna Schneller, *GQ*, October 1993.

"The guy was": "The Buzz on Johnny Depp," David Blum, *Esquire*, April 1995.

"On a scale": "Demolition Man," Christopher Hitchens, *People*, September 26, 1994.

"There's one thing": "Johnny Depp," Brendan Lemon, *Interview*, December 1995.

"It wasn't a great night": "The Buzz on Johnny Depp," David Blum, *Esquire*, April 1995.

"I can guarantee": "Playboy Interview: Johnny Depp," Kevin Cook, *Playboy*, January 1996.

Chapter 5

"Johnny said": "A Girl Called Kate," Shane Watson, British *Elle*, July 1995.

"They opened the curtains": "A Girl Called Kate," Shane Watson, British *Elle*, July 1995.

"I played him Barry White": "This Girl's Life," Steven Daly, *The Face*, May 1996.

"Well, when the publishers": "This Girl's Life," Steven Daly, *The Face*, May 1996.

"I don't know": *Kate: The Kate Moss Book*, Kate Moss, 1995.

"I did twenty-seven interviews": "All Grown Up," Tobias Peggs, *i-D*, September 1998.

"I'm uncomfortable with": "This Girl's Life," Steven Daly, *The Face*, May 1996.

"I had a really": "All Grown Up," Tobias Peggs, *i-D*, September 1998.

"Yeah. Who's going to": "Kate Moss," Avril Mair, *i-D*, December 1993.

"Moss is a very": "Selling the Woman-Child," John Leo, *U.S. News & World Report*, June 13, 1994.

"Well, after I did": "This Girl's Life," Steven Daly, *The Face*, May 1996.

"I love a Stoli": "The Thin Girl," Cathy Horyn, *Allure*, May 1994.

"The money": "This Girl's Life," Steven Daly, *The Face*, May 1996.

"[It] gets so": "What Katy Bought Next," Lisa Armstrong, British *Vogue*, April 1996.

"I love Kate": "Playboy Interview: Johnny Depp," Kevin Cook, *Playboy*, January 1996.

"I'm very true": "Playboy Interview: Johnny Depp," Kevin Cook, *Playboy*, January 1996.

"I am amazed": "Johnny Be Good," Kevin Sessums, *Vanity Fair*, February 1997.

"One of the producers": "Johnny Be Good," Darius James, *Vibe*, December 2001.

"She just thought": "Johnny Depp's Savage Journey," Chris Heath, *Rolling Stone*, June 11, 1998.

Chapter 6

"Everyone has that phase": "America's Obsession," Elizabeth Mitchell, *Spin*, January 1994.

"When we got": "Viva la Revolution," Jefferson Hack, *Dazed and Confused*, March 1999.

"We should stick": "Cannes Thriller: Gilliam vs. Godzilla," Bruce Kirkland, *Toronto Sun*, May 18, 1998.

"My room was next": "Kate Unmasked," Lisa Armstrong, British *Vogue*, April 1999.

"That's the sick thing": "Kate Unmasked," Lisa Armstrong, British *Vogue*, April 1999.

"No, I'm not": "All Grown Up," Tobias Peggs, *i-D*, September 1998.

"I actually had decoys": "Viva la Revolution," Jefferson Hack, *Dazed and Confused*, March 1999.

"What struck me": "An American in Paris," Gregory Katz, *USA Weekend*, July 4, 2003.

"That couldn't be": "Where's Johnny?" Johanna Schneller, *Premiere*, December 1999.

Chapter 7

"It was just a buildup": "The Kate Moss Story," Ingrid Sischy, *Interview*, March 1999.

"Kate's burned out": "Out of Fashion," Tresniowski, Blonska, Corcoran, Sanderson, Perry, Mooney, Fowler, Green, Miller, Summers, Stoynoff, Cojocaru, *People*, November 23, 1998.

"It was the best thing": "The Kate Moss Story," Ingrid Sischy, *Interview*, March 1999.

"Suddenly, it turned": "The Kate Review," Chris Heath, *The Face*, March 1999.

"It's kind of like": "Kate Unmasked," Lisa Armstrong, British *Vogue*, April 1999.

"I think he": "Kate Moss Gets Tossed Pink Slip for Calvin Klein Model," George Rush, Corky Siemaszko, *New York Daily News*, February 23, 1999.

"It was just amazing": "The Kate Moss Story," Ingrid Sischy, *Interview*, March 1999.

"I was quite": "Miss Moss," Bridget Foley, *W*, March 1999.

"I always said": "The Kate Review," Chris Heath, *The Face*, March 1999.

"It's like when": "Viva la Revolution," Jefferson Hack, *Dazed and Confused*, March 1999.

"He was away": "Kate Unmasked," Lisa Armstrong, British *Vogue*, April 1999.

"I don't think": "Viva la Revolution," Jefferson Hack, *Dazed and Confused*, March 1999.

"In France and London": "The Kate Review," Chris Heath, *The Face*, March 1999.

"Before, I was never": "The Face of the Decade," Nadene Ghouri, *The Big Issue*, January 2000.

Chapter 8

"You smell of pee": "Scent of a Woman," British *Vogue* Daily News Online, June 2001.

"When people come": "Creating Kate," Justine Picardie, British *Vogue*, May 2001.

"Kate always works": "Kate Unmasked," Lisa Armstrong, British *Vogue*, April 1999.

"You work": "The Kate Review," Chris Heath, *The Face*, March 1999.

bibliography

Alderman, Lesley. "Kate Moss [50 Most Beautiful People]," *People*,
    May 3, 1993.

Armstrong, Lisa. "Kate Unmasked," British *Vogue*, April 1999.

Armstrong, Lisa. "What Katy Bought Next," British *Vogue*, April
    1996.

Bainbridge, Simon. "The Face of Change," *British Journal of Photogra-
    phy*, March 31, 2004.

Barrett, Patrick. "Emap closes down *The Face*," media.guardian.co.uk,
    March 22, 2004.

Belcove, Julie L. "All About Kate," *W*, September 2003.

Blanchard, Tamsin. "This Year's Model," *The Observer*, August 26,
    2001.

Blum, David. "The Buzz on Johnny Depp," *Esquire*, April 1995.

Bride, Rachel. "How I Made It: Sarah Doukas, Founder of Storm
    Model Agency," *The Sunday Times* (UK), January 5, 2004.

Carter, Lee. "Shooting Stars in Focus: Fabien Baron," *Hint Mag*.

Cook, Kevin. "Playboy Interview: Johnny Depp," *Playboy*, January 1996.

corinneday.co.uk/bio.html

Daly, Steven. "This Girl's Life," *The Face*, May 1996.

d'Argy Smith, Marcelle. "Celebs to Blame for Anorexia," *Daily Mail*, October 2, 2003.

Farache, Emily. "Kate Moss Kidney Scare!" E! Online News, March 27, 2000.

Foley, Bridget. "Miss Moss," *W*, March 1999.

Foster, Jill. "Kate Looks 30 in the Face," *The Mirror*, January 13, 2004.

Gargett, Adrian. "Fast Times—the Photography of Corinne Day," getunderground.com, May 2003.

Garratt, Sheryl. "The Making of Kate," *The Face*, March 1993.

Gaudoin, Tina. "Little Miss Moss," *Harper's Bazaar*, December 1992.

Ghouri, Nadene. "The Face of the Decade," *The Big Issue*, January 2000.

Hack, Jefferson. "Viva la Revolution," *Dazed and Confused*, March 1999.

Heath, Chris. "Johnny Depp's Savage Journey," *Rolling Stone*, June 11, 1998.

Heath, Chris. "The Kate Review," *The Face*, March 1999.

hintmag.com/shootingstars/fabienbaron/fabienbaron1.htm

Hitchens, Christopher. "Demolition Man," *People*, September 26, 1994.

Horyn, Cathy. "The Thin Girl," *Allure*, May 1994.

J-files: "The Happy Mondays Background," Australian Broadcasting Corporation Online, December 14, 2000, abc.net.au/triplej/jfiles/files/s232051.htm

James, Darius. "Johnny Be Good," *Vibe*, February 1997.

"Kate Makes Quarter Century." British *Vogue Daily News Online*, January 1999.

Katz, Gregory. "An American in Paris," *USA Weekend*, July 4, 2003.

Keller, Julie. "Kate Moss: Model Mom," E! Online News, September 30, 2002.

Kirkland, Bruce. "Cannes Thriller: Gilliam vs. Godzilla," *Toronto Sun*, May 18, 1998.

Lague, Louise, et al. "How Thin Is Too Thin?" *People Weekly*, September 20, 1993.

Lee, Robinne. "Marky's Bad Rap?" *Tell* magazine, Summer 1994.

Lemon, Brendan. "Johnny Depp," *Interview*, December 1995.

Leo, John. "Selling the Woman-Child," *U.S. News & World Report*, June 13, 1994.

Mair, Avril. "Kate Moss," *i-D*, December 1993.

Mitchell, Elizabeth. "America's Obsession," *Spin*, January 1994.

models.com/model_culture/agency_spotlight/women

"Moss Be Some Mistake," British *Vogue Daily News Online*, June 1999.

Moss, Kate. *Kate: The Kate Moss Book*, Universe Publishing, 1995.

"Moss not Missus," British *Vogue Daily News Online*, August 1999.

Mower, Sarah. "Staying Alive," *Vogue*, September 2004.

"Out of Her Deppth," British *Vogue Daily News Online*, May 1999.

Parker, Ian. "Golden Girl," British *Esquire*, December 1993.

Peggs, Tobias. "All Grown Up," *i-D*, September 1998.

Picardie, Justine. "Creating Kate," British *Vogue*, May 2001.

Polhemus, Ted. *Street Style*, Thames & Hudson, 1994.

"Right Jesse," British *Vogue Daily News Online*, January 2000.

Rush, George, and Corky Siemaszko, "Kate Moss Gets Tossed Pink Slip for Calvin Klein Model," *New York Daily News*, February 23, 1999.

Ryan, James. "Depp Gets Deeper," *Vogue*, September 1994.

Schneller, Johanna. "Johnny Angel," *GQ*, October 1993.

Schneller, Johanna. "Where's Johnny?" *Premiere*, December 1999.

Sessums, Kevin. "Johnny Be Good," *Vanity Fair*, February 1997.

Sischy, Ingrid. "The Kate Moss Story," *Interview*, March 1999.

Sturino, Idella. "Breaking the Mold," *The Peak*, March 18, 1996.

Tresniowski, Alex, et al. "Out of Fashion," *People*, November 23, 1998.

Watson, Shane. "A Girl Called Kate," British *Elle*, July 1995.

Wayne, George. "Kiss Me, Kate," *Vanity Fair*, January 1994.

"What Katie Did," British *Vogue Daily News Online*, January 1999.

White, Lesley. "Small Wonder," British *Vogue*, August 1994.